SOUTHERN
ITALIAN
DESSERTS

SOUTHERN ITALIAN DESSERTS

Rediscovering the Sweet Traditions of
Calabria, Campania, Basilicata, Puglia, and Sicily

ROSETTA COSTANTINO

with Jennie Schacht

Photography by Sara Remington

TEN SPEED PRESS
Berkeley

To my children, Adrian and Danielle

Contents

Acknowledgments

I would never have written this book if not for my agent, Carole Bidnick, who asked me to write it. Many thanks to Celia Sack, owner of Omnivore Books on Food in San Francisco, California, who planted the idea for this cookbook in Carole's head. Special thanks to my editor at Ten Speed, Jenny Wapner, who believed in this book from the moment she first tasted my cannolo gelato, and to Andrea Chesman for her careful copyediting, and Betsy Stromberg for her enticing design.

Many thanks to Jennie Schacht for helping me with all the writing and for sharing her valuable knowledge of baking. Thanks to Randy Hicks, my cooking class assistant, for helping with editing the recipes and assisting with some challenging desserts. Thanks to photographer Sara Remington, who spent days driving with me all over Southern Italy to capture its beauty. She worked so hard with her food stylist, Katie Christ, and prop stylist, Dani Fisher, to make the food look gorgeous. Thanks to Holly Bern, Lisa Hanson, Rita Croda, Cyndi Wong, and Christina Kaelberer for testing my recipes and providing their constructive feedback.

I could not have written this book without the encouragement of my husband, Lino, and my children, Danielle and Adrian. My husband drove us thousands of miles all around Southern Italy during our summer vacation to whatever little town I requested in search of unknown sweets, keeping his sense of humor all the while. My son Adrian helped with testing all the recipes, tasting the desserts and providing his honest and constructive feedback, then bringing them to share with the wonderful teachers at his high school. I also thank my sister-in-law, Giuseppina Costantino, a physician in Palermo whose favorite hobby is baking desserts. Giuseppina shared many of the recipes that have added so much to this book.

I offer special thanks to the many Southern Italian people who offered their time, warm hospitality, and recipes: Pasquale Marigliano of San Gennariello di Ottaviano (Campania) allowed us to photograph him in his shop and demonstrated how to shape a *sfogliatella.* Manuela Piancastelli of Terre del Principe Agriturismo in Castel Campagnano (Campania) shared her recipe and introduced me to Pasquale. Antonio Cafiero of Gelateria Primavera in Sorrento (Campania) and his pastry chef, Silvana Parlato, showed me how to make the *delizie di limone* of Sorrento. Angie Cafiero introduced me to Antonio and shared her knowledge of the history of Neapolitan desserts. Massimiliano Avagliano, the pastry chef at Pasticceria Pantaleone in Salerno (Campania), shared his famous cake, the *scazzetta del cardinale.* Antonio Belcastro of Café Ninì in Diamante (Calabria) shared his *tartufo* recipe. Gaspare Abbate of La Cubana pastry shop in Palermo (Sicily) permitted us to photograph pastry chef Salvo La Porta making cannoli and *cassatelle.* Pasticceria Paradise in Palermo allowed us to take pictures of all their pastries. Maria Grammatico of her eponymous pastry shop in Erice (Sicily) spent time with us in her tiny shop and let us photograph her making her special almond pastries. Pietro Lecce of San Lorenzo Si Alberga and La Tavernetta restaurant in Camigliatello Silano (Calabria) shared his fig syrup recipe. Mary Taylor Simeti took time out of her busy schedule to share her vast knowledge of the history of Sicilian desserts. Patrick O'Boyle shared his family *pastiera* recipe. Many thanks to Rita Callipo of Agriturismo Casa Janca in Pizzo (Calabria), Margherita Amasino of Dattilo Ristorante in Strongoli (Calabria), Francesco Abbondanza of L'Abbondanza Lucana in Matera (Basilicata), Vincenzo Altieri of La Dolce Vita B&B in Matera, and to Laura Giordano, Antonello Losito, Roberto Bonanno, Giusi Di Benedetto, Silvana Bruno, Salvatore Germano and Anna Papa, and Italian food importer Rolando Beramendi. Many thanks to my cousins in Calabria: Vincenzo and Umberto Celia, Maria and Rosetta Torrano, and their families.

Finally, I thank my parents for giving me the greatest gift: teaching me everything they know about cooking.

An Introduction to Southern Italian Desserts

Southern Italy has a longstanding and well-deserved reputation for its lavish desserts, starting as early as 827 AD, when the Arabs first brought sugar to the area. Desserts here draw on a diversity of ingredients that reflect the area's long history of invasion and occupation by the Greeks, Romans, Byzantines, Lombards, Normans, Spanish, and French. Its location along the spice trading routes that crossed through the Mediterranean was fortuitous, bringing the exotic flavorings of far-away places to the region, including chocolate, cinnamon, and cloves. The Arabs and Spanish also brought almonds and pistachios, the latter originating in Syria, as well as *pasta reale* (marzipan)—used to fashion lifelike figurines of religious symbols, as well as miniature fruits and vegetables—and *pasta di mandorla* (almond paste, similar to but less sweet than marzipan), used in a variety of cookies.

Despite the riches brought by invading empires, until modern times elaborate sweets were found only in convents or by following the path of aristocrats—the only people who could afford the exorbitant price of sugar. Only at Christmastime might peasants have exchanged their goods for precious spices to flavor their simple cookies. Most often, desserts were made to honor a saint's day or a family occasion, such as a wedding or the birth of a child. To exalt those occasions, the desserts were made extra sweet, a characteristic still found in many Southern Italian desserts today.

Before the country's unification in 1860, Italy's capital shifted between Naples (Campania) and Palermo (Sicily), both important port cities. This meant these two cities developed some of the most extravagant desserts. It wasn't until the highway system was built after World War II that sugar and spices became widely available and affordable to ordinary Southern Italian families. Even today, Naples, Palermo, and Lecce (Puglia) are home to the area's most fanciful sweets. But dig further and you will find a wealth of simpler but equally delicious desserts throughout Southern Italy, dreamed up by resourceful home cooks using the ingredients and tools available to them.

Evolution of the Southern Italian Pastry Shop

Before the advent of pastry shops, most sweets made at home were simple cookies that could be made and stored without refrigeration. Most were sweetened with the liqueurs made in many homes, with the dried fruit of the fig trees that grow all over the region, or with syrups like honey and *mosto cotto,* made by boiling down the juice of wine grapes. These treats were labor intensive and certainly not an everyday extravagance.

Beginning in the late 1800s, a wave of Swiss immigrants came to Southern Italy seeking respite from the economic crisis taking place in their home country; they soon became Southern Italy's largest immigrant population. Among them were pastry chefs who chose the areas of Naples and Palermo, knowing that local aristocrats would make good customers for their sophisticated sweets. With this Swiss influx came cream, butter, and new baking techniques. Before that time, lard was the primary fat used in baking. The Caflisch family, well known throughout Southern Italy, emigrated from Switzerland and opened pastry shops in Naples, where they introduced many of the miniature pastries, tartlets, and other desserts associated with the area today. Soon they expanded their operations and influence to Palermo, Catania (Sicily), and Brindisi (Puglia), a coastal town at the heel of the boot. In Palermo, one still finds fancy bakeries designated *pasticceria Svizzera,* or Swiss pastry shop, where locals shop for beautifully wrapped boxes of confections as gifts to auger sweetness. Elsewhere in Southern Italy, the *pasticcerie* are busiest on Sundays and holidays, where customers point to pastries displayed in long showcases, the clerks busily boxing up the sweets to be taken home and enjoyed as part of the meal following church. Even today, it is rare to find these kinds of opulent pastries prepared in the home.

It was the cloistered nuns, largely in Sicily, Campania, Lecce, and Bari (another Puglia coastal town), who refined many Southern Italian confections. From the Middle Ages, monasteries housed equipment used to make sweets for clergy and nobles. While living at the convent, the nuns had time to fashion elaborate desserts that would have been impractical to make in private homes, providing the community a source of rich pastries purchased through a small convent window and the monasteries with needed funds to support their religious mission. Each monastery had its own specialty, the recipe closely guarded. When nuns occasionally left the monasteries, they took these tightly held kitchen secrets with them, eventually leaking them out into the communities where they settled. Many of these sweets eventually became pastry shop mainstays.

Some will tell you that another iconic Southern Italian sweet, gelato, was invented in Paris. The credit rightly belongs to Francesco Procopio dei Coltelli, a Sicilian living in Paris, who introduced gelato to Parisian cafe society. In fact, gelato has its roots in snow, which the Romans enjoyed topped with fruit juices as a refreshing treat. These days, ice cream shops are found throughout Italy. Sicily has the distinction of serving the frozen treat with whipped cream and stuffed inside a brioche bun. (You'll find locals in Reggio Calabria enjoying *brioche con gelato* as well.)

Regional Differences

If you visit private homes and pastry shops today across the five regions covered in this book, you will notice a curious thing: alongside regional specialties and the most popular desserts from Palermo and Naples, many similar cookies are found throughout this large area, with only slight variations in their ingredients, shapes, and names. These variations on common sweets harken back to recipes brought through Greek and Roman occupations, adapted by towns and even individual families to suit their available ingredients and tastes, and named in the local dialects that have evolved through the mingling of languages.

Italian cuisine is strongly regional, with many foods associated with a specific area. Even from town to town, the same food might be made with a local twist, and desserts are no different. In each area, primarily a few local ingredients are used—ricotta, honey, and pistachios in Sicily; lemons, amarena cherries, and ricotta in Campania; figs and citrus in Calabria; almonds and *mosto cotto* in Puglia; and walnuts, chestnuts, honey, and chickpeas in Basilicata. Creative pastry cooks have found ways to transform these few ingredients into an impressive array of treats.

As a child, I assumed that the few desserts we knew were particular to our town of Verbicaro (Calabria), so I was surprised in my more recent travels to find similar or sometimes even identical formulations in other parts of Southern Italy. When a dessert travels from one region to another, it will typically adopt a name in local dialect, and it will be made with a slightly different formula, finished with a filling made from locally available ingredients, or formed in a new shape, often with symbolic meaning, remembering a historical event or fable, or representing an aspect of religious belief.

Holidays Are a Time for Sweets

All across Italy, Christmas is the most important holiday of the year and, as with all things Italian, countless holiday traditions are focused on the table. Meals are punctuated with abundant sweets, many eaten only once a year on a designated occasion, and many found only in a particular town.

The winter celebrations begin well in advance of Christmas, with Calabrians and Sicilians celebrating the Festa di Santa Lucia on December 13 by eating bowls of *la cuccia,* a long-cooked wheat berry pudding perked up with ricotta cream or nuts and *mosto cotto.* The holiday marks the miraculous arrival in Palermo of a ship with grain, answering the prayers of the starving locals to Santa Lucia.

All Southern Italian towns have a Christmas tradition involving a sweetened, fried dough coated with honey or *mosto cotto,* originating from Greek culture and harkening back to a time when most families had a fire to heat oil, but few had ovens in their home, instead sharing communal wood-burning ovens. Other Christmas desserts date back to early Roman days, when Saturnalia, the winter solstice, was celebrated at this time. Over the years, Christian culinary customs have evolved to incorporate pagan traditions, and many Christmas desserts are found in shapes related to Saturnalia: *scalidde* (or *scalille*) of sweet fritters shaped as a ladder ascending toward the heavens, and the *luna* (moon) shape are examples. In Puglia and Basilicata, fried rosettes of a similar sweet dough are known as *cartellate* and are served coated with *mosto cotto* or honey.

In the Cosenza region of Calabria, where I come from, Christmas brings plates piled high with the warm yeasted fritters called *grispelle* (elsewhere called *zeppole*) drizzled with the local honey. *Turdilli* and *cannariculi* are other Calabrian Christmas traditions, as is *pitta 'mpigliata,* pastry rosettes filled with a mixture of walnuts, raisins, and cinnamon.

In Reggio Calabria, the southernmost part in Calabria, the Christmas table is heaped with the chocolate-glazed half-moon turnovers called *petrali,* filled with dried figs, nuts, citron, and orange zest, flavored with chocolate, and bound together with *mosto cotto.* Also popular are *pignolata,* tiny fritters the size of a chickpea glazed with lemon or chocolate icing. My in-laws in Palermo make

buccellato, a ring-shaped pastry filled with dried figs. The Christmas fig cookies known as *cucciddati* are found throughout Sicily.

Although Christmas is the most widely celebrated holiday in Southern Italy, it is by no means the only time at which sweets flood the table. For the feast of Carnevale, preceding Lent, Southern Italians celebrate with pieces of sweet dough shaped into bows or strips, fried, and dusted heavily with confectioners' sugar. These cookies are meant to tattle on those who sneak off with one by virtue of the trail of powdered sugar they leave in their wake. Depending on the town in which you find them, the cookies may be called *chiacchiere* (chit-chatters) or *bugie* (liars). Chickpea-size *cicirata* and *migliaccio* show up at this time of year as well. There would be no Sicilian Carnevale if not for their world-famous cannoli. This is also the time of the year when *sanguinaccio* is prepared in homes, made from fresh pig's blood mixed with chocolate, bread crumbs, nuts, and spices, baked into a rich crostata. It's a local specialty that, though I didn't include a recipe here, is much tastier than you might imagine!

During Pasqua, the Italian Easter, hard-cooked eggs are baked into sweet breads in remembrance of Christ's resurrection, auguring new life in the coming spring. Like many sweets, the names given these breads depend on where you find them: *scarcelle* in Puglia, *cuzzuppe* in Calabria, *pannaredde* in Basilicata, and *pupu cu l'uovu* in Sicily. Home cooks in Campania prepare *pastiera,* a tart made from cooked wheat berries, which has also become popular in other areas, including my native region of Calabria. In Sicily, the dome-shaped *cassata*, lined with sponge cake, soaked in liqueur, filled with ricotta, and covered with marzipan and candied fruits, takes center stage. Its name is believed to have been derived from the Arab word *quas'at,* denoting its round shape.

Every town throughout Italy has a patron saint, each with its own saint's day, or *festa.* Most of the *feste* are celebrated in summer, but whatever the time of year, sweets always play a role in the celebration. Each town celebrates their patron saint with a Sunday procession, where townspeople parade a life-size replica of their beloved saint through the streets. Following the parade, families return home to tables laid out with special foods, ending with sweets often reserved for that one special day. Many of the desserts in this book come from these holiday traditions.

Southern Italian Desserts through My Eyes

As I was growing up, dessert was strictly reserved for feast days and special occasions—perhaps a baptism, communion, or birthday celebration. For most of my childhood, if we had dessert at all, it was a simple piece of fresh fruit, or the combination of cut-up fruits known in Italy as *macedonia.* My mother made just one type of candy, similar to the single sweet she knew as a child: dried figs, sometimes cut open and stuffed with a piece of walnut, shaped into a *crocette* (cross) or *coroncine* (wreath), then baked to preserve them through the winter months. She would also make plain *taralli* cookies, *visquotti* in our dialect, in our wood-burning oven, adding eggs and coating them with a sugar glaze to dress them up for Easter. During the year, the plain, slightly sweetened *taralli* accompanied our morning coffee.

When I was eight, a woman from Salerno (Campania) opened the first pastry shop in my remote corner at the toe of the boot. I walked by this *pasticceria* on the way to and from school, and when I had 200 lire or so in my pocket, I'd pick up a treat. As I got older, my mother expanded her repertoire to include a single cake: *pan di Spagna,* a plain sponge cake raised through the prolonged beating of eggs to incorporate air, which she accomplished by holding together two dinner forks as a kind of makeshift whisk. Other than the pan used to bake that cake, we had no baking tools to speak of. The cakes were baked in our wood-burning oven once a hand extended into the oven sensed that the temperature was about right. At that point, my mother, aunt, and neighbors would bake four or five of these cakes for their families.

My mother never saw a dessert filled with pastry cream until after she was married, when she had the chance to sample her brother-in-law's *sospiri* (sighs)—delicate individual sponge cakes filled with cream, drowned in sugary icing, and topped with a cherry. The sweets she knew as a child were mostly traditional holiday desserts, typically a sweet fried dough coated with honey. Her candies were those dried figs stuffed with a piece of walnut, or *panicelli*—little bundles of dried muscat raisins flavored with citron, wrapped in citron leaves, and baked. Gently sweetened *taralli* were the basic cookies, as they were in my youth, typical throughout Calabria, Basilicata, and Puglia.

As children, my parents' families packed snow into a bowl, sweetening and flavoring it with *mosto cotto* or orange juice. In the days before refrigeration, during summer, people in my town would go out on ice-finding expeditions, retrieving huge blocks from an area between two mountain peaks at 6,000 feet that never saw the sun. They would find it there all the way into August, bringing back the huge slabs for making ice cream. Refrigeration came to our area in the late 1950s, and I was fortunate to have gelato from the time I was young.

As ice cream and pastry shops later proliferated in the area, we learned about all kinds of desserts. I loved the *bomboloni* (cream-filled doughnuts) and *sfogliatelle* (rich filled pastries) sold at these shops. But I never considered that they could be made at home, and even as I developed the recipes in this book, I was surprised to find that many of these revered recipes were not only possible, but often easy to prepare in a home kitchen.

About This Book

I have organized the desserts of Southern Italy by region, with each chapter showcasing my favorites from among the area's typical desserts and, occasionally, modern interpretations now found there. Representing the broad expanse of what you would find traveling through Sicily, Campania, Calabria, Puglia, and Basilicata, the recipes range from simple home desserts to the cutting-edge creations of Southern Italy's finest restaurants and pastry shops. I've included desserts already well known and loved in America, such as gelato and cannoli, as well as regional specialties virtually unknown in this country and rarely, if ever, found in books, magazines, or online. The almond cookies filled with cherry preserves called *Biscotti di Ceglie,* a typical sweet in one of Puglia's oldest towns, or the ricotta and semolina cake made for Carnevale in Naples called *Il Migliaccio* may be found in Italian cookbooks and on Italian websites, but to my knowledge these have not been heretofore available in English. Others, such as the *Biscotti Eureka, Africano,* and *Foglie da Te',* I found in pastry shops while traveling through the region, returning to decipher cryptic advice from pastry chefs to reproduce them. These have been some of my favorites to develop, crowned by the satisfaction of creating something that looks and tastes utterly authentic, or even better than the original.

I have shared here only a small sample of the thousands of recipes enjoyed in Southern Italy. My dearest hope is that not only will you make and enjoy them in your home, but that you might consider visiting and falling in love with this magical area that offers my most cherished sweets (and savory foods, as well). The desserts found in homes, pastry shops, *gelaterie,* and restaurants still surprise and delight me, and I find something both comforting and familiar, yet new and exciting, each time I return. This book is meant to bring these desserts—many of which are found in the United States primarily among Italian populations, if at all—into our common lexicon, preserving them for future generations. It is my invitation to you to share in the sweetness of my favorite desserts.

An Invitation

I was delighted when my agent asked that I consider filling a void she noticed: no good English-language book was in publication on Southern Italian desserts. As I teach Southern Italian cooking classes and had already written *My Calabria,* she thought I was the one to do it. I hesitated at first because I have no training as a pastry chef and I could hardly believe that no such book existed. After doing some research, both in the United States and in Italy, I found no single book spanning the desserts of this intriguing area, so I began to re-create some of my best-loved pastries from my Calabrian childhood. In the process, I discovered a world of sweets I had never known, inspiring me to collect my old and new favorites in this volume, including many I was unable to find documented (or well documented) in English. It was a challenge to limit the book to the seventy-six desserts and master recipes found here, and there are many others I wish I could have included. I've learned so much along the way, perhaps most importantly this: if I am able to make these desserts in my own kitchen, I know you can, too, from those requiring only my mother's tools back in Italy—a bowl and a fork—to the most challenging, which I've made every effort to simplify with clear instructions and photographs to show you the way. I hope you'll join me in the Southern Italian pastry kitchen.

A Southern Italian Dessert Pantry

It is astounding to think of the modest Calabrian kitchen of my childhood compared to the vast resources I now have at my disposal in my Oakland, California, home. Yet, with hardly more than a bowl, a couple of forks, and a wood-burning oven, my mother was able to transform a few simple ingredients into a moist, eggy *pan di Spagna* as light as air. It was delightful enough on its own. Soaked in the local liqueur and dressed up with cream and fruit, it was ethereal.

As a child this feat seemed magical. As an adult with the consistent ingredients, electronic scale, stand mixer with multiple attachments, heat-resistant silicone spatulas, and calibrated electric oven I have at my disposal today, it seems nearly inconceivable that she pulled off this trick using a simple baking pan and a wood-burning oven with no thermometer.

For many of the desserts in this book, all that is needed are a few simple ingredients and the minimal equipment used by the *nonne* of Southern Italy. However, a few modern conveniences will make your work lighter and your results more reliable. The equipment and ingredients that follow will have you well prepared for any of the recipes in the book, from simple home desserts to those made in the finest *pasticcerie.*

Equipment

Baking sheets. I used 18- by 12-inch heavy-gauge aluminum baking sheets, both rimmed and rimless, to create and test the recipes in this book. Look for sturdy, light-colored baking sheets because the flimsy ones easily warp, and the darker-colored sheets may result in overbrowning your cookie bottoms. For the rimless sheets, I recommend insulated ones for even baking.

Blender. My powerful Blendtec blender produces smooth nut pastes, like *pasta di nocciola* (page 192) and *pasta di pistacchio* (page 190). In most cases, a good-quality blender or food processor will do the job, though they may not produce quite as smooth a paste.

Cake pans, tart pans, and springform pans. Most of the recipes call for an 8-, 9-, or 10-inch round cake pan with 2- to 3-inch tall sides. Where it makes it easier to unmold the cake, I prefer a springform pan of similar size. Tart pans with removable bottoms also make easy work of removing a crostata from the pan, leaving it on the base for serving. In most cases a springform pan will perform as well, though the taller sides may slightly increase the baking time.

Cannoli forms. Look in cookware shops, Italian specialty shops, or online (see Sources, page 203) for metal forms on which to wrap your cannoli pastry for frying. I make my forms the old-fashioned way, using the reed called *Arundo donax,* similar to the traditional bamboo-like canes from which the pastry takes its name. If it grows in your area, where it might be known as Giant Cane or Giant Reed, you can make cannoli forms by cutting the reeds between their knots into 6-inch segments.

Electric mixer. My KitchenAid 5-quart stand mixer allows me to have the mixer running while I step away to measure and prepare ingredients and perform other tasks. If you have one, an extra bowl and whisk attachment are handy for easily switching to a clean bowl and beaters for whipping egg whites. In most cases, a handheld electric mixer will do the job, though you will have to hold it as you beat.

Electric multipurpose cooker, deep fryer, or electric frying pan. A deep, heavy pot and a thermometer is all you need for recipes that require frying, but an electric cooker will make it easier to regulate the heat and will simplify cleanup.

Ice cream maker. I use a Cuisinart ICE-21 ice cream maker with a 6-cup capacity, the type that requires chilling a coolant-filled canister in the freezer. I keep my canister frozen at all times, but if space is short you will want to freeze it for at least 24 hours before spinning your ice cream. Alternatively, an old-fashioned ice cream machine, in which you pack the area around the ice cream canister with ice and rock salt, also works well. They can be found in both electric and hand-churn models.

Parchment paper and silicone baking mats. Lining your pans makes for a much easier and more reliable release when it comes time to unmold a cake or transfer cookies to a wire rack to cool. I purchase parchment paper precut to fit a variety of baking pans and sheets, but you can easily cut parchment from the roll to fit your pans. Silicone baking mats also work well and can be reused hundreds of times, simply wiping them clean between uses. I use both.

Pasta machine. A pasta machine makes easy work of forming thin pastry sheets for *Sfogliatelle Ricce, Chiacchiere,* cannoli shells, *Cartellate,* and *Canzoncelli.* Where the pasta machine is used, I offer alternative instructions using a rolling pin.

Pastry bag and tips. These plastic or lined bags are handy for piping pastries such as *zeppole* and for filling pastries. Look for 12- to 14-inch bags for most tasks. I keep plain round tips on hand in several sizes, as well as a couple of open star tips. You won't need anything much fancier for the recipes in this book. For piping heavy batters and doughs, I prefer to use large tips, which can be dropped directly into the pastry bag. Fitted snugly into the opening, these heavy tips stay in place without the two-piece plastic coupler typically used to hold the tip in place. For finer work, such as decorating, I use smaller tips and a coupler.

Pastry cutters. These are handy for cutting pastry in straight lines, by first marking it and then rolling the cutter across the dough. Fluted cutters make for pretty edges but are not essential.

Scale. More than any other piece of equipment on this list, I highly recommend keeping a scale in your kitchen. It needn't be fancy or expensive so long as it is calibrated, shows weights in either grams or ounces, and can be tared (set back to zero) when you add each new ingredient. Especially with baking, cooking by weight is much more precise, produces more reliable results, and is easier and neater than using measuring cups.

Spatulas, icing. An offset metal icing spatula is useful for smoothing and leveling cake tops and icings. I keep both the larger (7- to 8-inch) and smaller (4-inch) sizes on hand.

Spatulas, scrapers. I use heatproof silicone spatulas for stirring mixtures as I heat them, and also for folding ingredients together or scraping a batter into a pan.

Strainers: medium-, fine-, and ultrafine-mesh and wire-mesh splatter screens. For most straining tasks, I use a medium-mesh strainer. For straining out small solids, such as berry seeds, a fine-mesh strainer is also helpful. I press ricotta through a flat ultrafine splatter screen using a firm but flexible plastic bowl scraper to make a smooth ricotta cream. The screen is the type meant to be placed over a pan when frying. They're not expensive, and it's well worth having one on hand, even if only for this one task.

Thermometer. I use a digital instant-read thermometer to check the temperature of baked custards and of milk when making ricotta. A candy thermometer is the best one to monitor the heat of oil for frying. Calibrate your thermometer using a properly made ice bath: Fill a glass to the rim with ice (crushed is best) and add just enough cold tap water to fill in the gaps between the ice, stopping one-half inch short of the top of the ice. The ice should not float. Let stand one minute, then insert the thermometer tip two inches into the water and stir. The thermometer should read within one degree of 32°F (0°C).

Whisks. It's worth having whisks on hand in many sizes. The two I use most are a large balloon whisk for whipping air into eggs and cream, and a medium-size straight whisk for stirring custards and other mixtures smooth.

Zesters. I can hardly remember life before the Microplane rasp-style grater. I use these for zesting lemons and oranges, and they come in sizes meant for making piles of fine chocolate curls, grating nutmeg, and a variety of other tasks.

It is also helpful to have the following supplies on hand in your kitchen:
- Cooling racks
- Food processor (both a full-size and mini processor are useful)
- Measuring cups and spoons
- Mixing bowls
- Pastry brushes
- Rolling pin
- Ruler or tape measure, for measuring rolled dough, cutting precise shapes, and similar tasks.

Ingredients

Candied orange peel. Oranges grow throughout Southern Italy, and their candied peel is a mainstay of Southern Italian desserts, including the ones in this book. In fact, I call for them in my recipes so frequently that I urge you to make your own (page 193) to

keep on hand. I have tried many store-bought examples but nothing comes close to the ones you can make yourself. Though it takes a bit of time, it's not at all difficult. The peels store well, so I make them just once a year and use them all year long. If you do not make your own, seek out the best quality candied peel you can find, avoiding at all cost the hard, bright-colored, fake-looking (and fake-tasting) diced candied peels sold in tubs on supermarket shelves. If that's all you can find, I'd rather you left them out of the recipes. Southern Italians also use candied citron, a nearly juiceless citrus fruit prized for its peel. In the Unites States, I've seen it only in New York City's Little Italy, but if you can find the large, bumpy-fleshed, light green candied citron imported from Italy called *cedro candito,* nab it—you've found the real thing.

Chocolate. I am a chocoholic, and my favorite chocolate is dark, at least 55 percent to about 70 percent cacao. (Where cacao percentage matters, I've specified ranges in the recipes.) While I have my own preferred brands, the best chocolate is the one you like, so taste many varieties and discover what you like best. I use Valrhona chocolate for baking, but any good chocolate will do.

Cocoa powder. My favorite cocoa powder is also the deep, dark Valrhona, but for these recipes you may choose any unsweetened alkalized (Dutch-processed) cocoa powder you like. The ones typically used in Southern Italy are similar to my beloved Valrhona.

Eggs. The eggs called for in my recipes are always large, weighing approximately 2 ounces (60 g) with the shell and measuring 3 to 4 tablespoons (about 50 g) cracked, of which the yolk is about 1 tablespoon (20 g) and the white 2 tablespoons (30 g). Use the freshest eggs you can find—these recipes were all tested using supermarket eggs, but I much prefer using the eggs from my backyard chickens, with their brilliant yellow yolks.

Extracts. In Italy, rather than using extracts most people bake with vanilla-flavored sugar, found in small packets labeled *zucchero vanigliato,* or they use whole vanilla beans. Here, I find vanilla extract gives the most consistent results. Choose a pure (not imitation), good-quality extract. Likewise, use pure almond and orange extracts. They may be pricey, but you'll need only a small amount and the flavor is infinitely better.

Fats. When I was growing up in Calabria, lard and olive oil were the fats of choice for pastry making. Known in Italy as *strutto* (or *sugna* in dialect), lard is made by rendering pork fat, which, once cooled to a firm consistency, may be used like butter. If you wish to use lard in the recipes where it is offered as an option, ask your local butcher shop if they produce or carry a good-quality leaf lard. Please avoid the hydrogenated lard sold in supermarkets, which often has an off taste. In some of the recipes traditionally made with lard in Italy, I have substituted butter because it is more readily available and produces good results. Always use unsalted butter so that you can control the amount of salt in the recipe. For olive oil, look for a good-quality extra-virgin oil with a fresh, buttery taste because the flavor will come through in your desserts. For deep-frying, use a neutral-tasting vegetable oil with a high smoking point, such as safflower or sunflower.

Flour. I use unbleached all-purpose flour in most of my recipes. When specified, cake flour is used to more closely match Italian recipes, which often include a small amount of potato starch. Flour is one of the most difficult ingredients to measure accurately, and even small differences can affect the outcome of your desserts. For the best and most consistent results, weigh rather than measure your flour. If you don't have a scale, measure it using dry measuring cups—the kind that you fill to the rim, rather than the spouted glass measuring cups meant for liquids. Begin by stirring the flour in the bag or canister to loosen it. Holding the cup over the sack or canister of flour, spoon in the flour to overflowing, then scrape the back of a table knife straight across the rim of the cup to remove the excess flour.

Gelatin. Gelatin is sold in sheets, also called leaves, as well as powdered in small packets. I prefer the sheets because they dissolve more readily and are easy to squeeze out and transfer from a small bowl of liquid to the recipe ingredients without adding excess liquid. The sheets are graded gold, silver, or bronze from strongest to weakest. The average-strength silver works well in most recipes; bronze should work well, too. Gold is too strong for these recipes.

If you substitute gelatin powder for gelatin sheets, allow it to "bloom" by evenly sprinkling the powder over a small bowl of cool liquid. Allow it to hydrate for about 5 minutes before stirring it into the warm recipe ingredients. One envelope of gelatin powder contains $1/4$ ounce (7 g), roughly equivalent to four silver gelatin sheets.

Honey. Because the bees in Southern Italy often feed on the area's pervasive orange blossoms, *miele di zagara,* or orange blossom honey, is the type most commonly used in Southern Italian baking. Also common is *mille fiori,* similar to our wildflower honey. You can substitute another mild honey, such as acacia or clover, but avoid strong-flavored ones, such as chestnut, which would overpower the dessert.

Liqueurs. Italians love their liqueurs and frequently use them to flavor desserts. Strega is the herb-based liqueur from Benevento, in Campania, colored yellow from saffron and the mix of more than seventy herbs. Maraschino is a cherry liqueur used to soak cakes and to flavor *macedonia di frutta* (fruit salad); I use Luxardo

brand. Made with the local lemons, limoncello is also frequently used in Southern Italian baking. Make your own (page 200) or purchase an Italian brand; the best come from Sorrento or elsewhere on the Amalfi Coast.

Nuts. Many Southern Italian pastries are based on the nuts grown in the area, which include almonds, hazelnuts, pistachios, walnuts, and pine nuts. For the freshest nuts, purchase them raw in bulk from a store with frequent turnover, sampling a couple before you buy. Because their high oil content tends to turn nuts rancid when stored at room temperature, I store mine in the freezer.

To toast nuts, place them on a baking sheet and toast in a preheated 350°F (177°C) oven for 10 to 15 minutes, until they darken and smell toasty.

Pistachio paste. This paste is made by grinding pistachios with a small amount of vegetable oil until completely smooth and almost pourable. Sicilians also use a sweetened version in their desserts called *crema di pistacchio*, which is sometimes enriched with milk or cocoa butter. Sold in jars, the *crema* is difficult to make properly at home. Instead, choose an Italian brand, such as Fiasconaro Oro Verde Bronte Pistachio Cream, available on Amazon.com, or Villa Reale, available from Market Hall Foods (see Sources, page 203).

Ricotta. For the recipes in this book, you will have the best results using the homemade ricotta on page 186. If you prefer to purchase ricotta, look for a top-quality whole-milk ricotta such as Calabro, Angelo & Franco, or Bellwether brands. On the East Coast, you may find fresh ricotta made by local Italians in shops, the closest thing you can purchase to making your own. If you have never made ricotta yourself, I encourage you to give it a try!

Ricotta for the recipes in this book should always be well drained in advance of preparing the recipe. This is especially important when using store-bought ricotta, which tends to retain more liquid than homemade. To drain the ricotta, put it into a cheesecloth-lined strainer over a bowl to catch the dripping whey. Cover the top with plastic wrap and refrigerate overnight, discarding the whey in the morning.

Salt. I use kosher salt in all of my cooking and baking. The salt is not actually kosher, but rather is named for its role in making meats kosher. I like the salt for its larger crystal size and its clean taste. To substitute fine sea salt, use half as much as the recipes indicate. I do not recommend using table salt, which includes additives that adversely affect its flavor.

Sugar. I use granulated sugar in the recipes unless I specify confectioners' (powdered) sugar. When using confectioners' sugar, sift it before using to remove lumps. Granulated and confectioners' sugars are not interchangeable.

1

Sicilia

Sicily is an extraordinary island of great natural beauty and historic importance. It is a place where churches decorated with elaborate mosaics and some of the world's most striking Greek and Roman ruins stand against a backdrop of rugged coastline, sparkling sea, quaint fishing villages, and the volcanic snow-capped Mount Etna. Gardens are resplendent not only with flowers, but also with citrus and olive trees. Vines produce grapes used to make wines both dry and sweet.

Among the many cultures that have occupied Sicily over the centuries, the Arabs ruled the island for more than one hundred years, until they were defeated by the Normans in the early eleventh century. Of the island's many occupants, it is the Arabs who left the most lasting mark on Sicily's pastries. They planted pistachio trees in Bronte, at the foot of Mount Etna, and brought sugar, cinnamon, almond paste, and sesame, all still widely used to prepare Sicilian sweets.

Many Sicilian desserts originated in convents, which are said to have competed fiercely against one another, each vying to craft the most elaborate sweets to gain favor with the priests. As word got out about their creations, the nuns began to sell them to the public as a means of funding church activities. Many details of this history have been lost as the nuns have passed away, but it is believed that well-to-do families would marry off their first daughter, resigning the others to the convent to avoid paying additional dowries or having to divide their precious land among many sons-in-law, risking loss of their property title. These well-heeled, well-educated girls had been introduced to pastry making at home, and thus brought these skills with them to the convents. In her book *Bitter Almonds,* Mary Taylor Simeti recounts the childhood of Sicily's best-known pastry maker, Maria Grammatico, who parlayed an arduous life in one of these convent orphanages into her world-renowned eponymous pastry shop perched high in the hilltop town of Erice.

To step into a Palermo pastry shop today is to be swept off your feet by evocative scents, brilliant colors, and opulent displays of pastries. You can almost read the area's history in these desserts, which reflect the diverse cultures that have controlled the island over time—Phoenician, Greek, Roman, Arab, Byzantine, Norman, French, Spanish, and Bourbon—yet which have somehow melded into a harmonious mix of textures and flavors unique to Sicily.

Because my husband's family is from this area, I have often traveled there and have sampled many of the area's typical pastries. From my own family members who still live there, I have learned that today's Sicilian desserts are derived from three main sources: peasant women, relied on to provide sweets for their families for every religious festival or major family holiday; convents, where nuns prepared rich and intricate desserts as part of their monastic charge; and talented Swiss pastry chefs who came to the island in the late 1800s. Chefs such as those from the Caflisch family first opened shops in Naples, then moved to Palermo, opening shops there as well, and later opened shops throughout Sicily and on the mainland. These *pasticcerie Svizzere* (Swiss pastry shops) have since become integrated into the Sicilian pastry shops, and like my husband's uncle, most of the pastry chefs were originally trained in the Swiss methods, using them to fashion many of the newer desserts now associated with the island.

As in many parts of Italy, Sicilian provinces celebrate festivals and religious events with their own traditional sweets. In some cases, the desserts are similar but are known by different names in the local dialect. Throughout Sicily, perhaps the holidays most associated with sweets are Easter and All Souls' Day. For Easter, eggs, sugar, marzipan, and ricotta are crafted into shapes with distinct religious or symbolic meanings related to springtime and rebirth. As in other parts of Southern Italy, whole hard-cooked eggs are baked into breads at this time, but here, the pastry is given the name, in dialect, *u pupu cu l'uovu,* or "the doll with the egg," and is also molded into baskets or dove shapes. Marzipan is formed into the paschal lamb, *la pecorella di Pasqua.* Perhaps Sicily's best-

known dessert, the *cassata,* originated with the Arabs, but only in the Baroque era were these cakes transformed into artistic masterpieces, elaborately decorated with candied fruit. Though it is now found year-round as a signature Palermo sweet, it is considered the quintessential Easter cake.

Festa dei Morti, or All Souls' Day, is celebrated in Palermo on November 2 and, similar to our Halloween, it is a child-focused day of celebration. As a child in Palermo, my husband eagerly awaited this holiday, when returning souls brought him toys and sweets like *ossi di morti* or *tetu* cookies, as well as the marzipan-shaped fruits called *frutta martorana,* named for the convent La Martorana, where the nuns developed special skills in molding and painting marzipan into lifelike representations of fruits and figurines. Today, bakeries throughout Sicily display baskets of these fruits, which may cause you to do a double-take when you realize that they are crafted from *pasta reale* (almond paste) and are not the real thing.

Some desserts are still found only on a particular holiday and not at other times of year. *Cuccia* (page 49), the simple spoon dessert made from cooked wheat berries and sweetened ricotta, is the only form in which wheat is eaten during the Festa di Santa Lucia, celebrated in Palermo on December 13, in remembrance of the arrival of wheat to the port in answer to the farmers' prayers. Variations of *cuccia* are found throughout the island.

St. Joseph's Day is celebrated on March 19, when the dessert of the day is a fried pastry called *Sfince di San Giuseppe* (page 58). How you will find them shaped and filled will depend on where you are joining in the celebration; in Palermo, they are filled with ricotta cream.

The most common Christmas dessert is the *buccellato,* a large, wreath-shaped pastry filled with dried figs and nuts. *Cucciddati*, small cookies with a similar filling, are popular throughout the island.

Besides *cassata* and cannoli, the dessert most commonly associated with Sicily is gelato, thickened here with cornstarch or wheat starch instead of egg yolks, and made with more milk than cream. In summer, you will find Sicilians heading down the street to work with a gelato-filled brioche in hand, a sort of ice cream breakfast sandwich, or enjoying the same as an afternoon pick-me-up. The Arabs brought Sicily its refreshing granita, a popular refreshment in the hot summers. Though it is named for the grains of flavored ice scraped up into piles as the mixture freezes, in modern times you will find it frozen into a smooth, almost creamy texture, like sorbet, and flavored with a variety of fruits, as well as in coffee, chocolate, almond, jasmine, and other local flavors. A similar summer refreshment is *Gelo di Mellone* (page 60), a chilled pudding made from watermelon juice and decorated with bits of chocolate and pistachio, associated with the celebration of Palermo's patron saint, Rosalia.

Pasticcini di Mandorla soft almond cookies

These little almond cookies are found all over Sicily and often in other parts of Southern Italy as well. They are pretty piped with a star tip into rosettes or into "S" shapes, but you needn't be adept at piping; more often they are simply formed into balls and rolled either in confectioners' sugar or chopped nuts before baking, as I have done here.

To pipe the cookies, spoon the dough into a pastry bag fitted with a star tip (Ateco #826), or use a ziplock bag and cut a $^{1}/_{2}$-inch opening in one corner. Refrigerate the dough for an hour to help the cookies hold their shape when piped and baked, then pipe thirty-six cookies onto the prepared baking sheet. Sprinkle the tops lightly with granulated sugar and lightly press a whole blanched almond, candied cherry, or piece of candied orange peel into the tops before baking.

$1^{2}/_{3}$ cups (250 g) blanched almonds (page 189)

1 cup (200 g) granulated sugar

2 large egg whites

2 tablespoons mild-flavored honey, such as clover or orange blossom

$^{1}/_{4}$ teaspoon pure almond extract

Confectioners' sugar, finely chopped pistachios or hazelnuts, sliced almonds, or whole pine nuts, for coating

Preheat the oven to 350°F (177°C) with a rack in the center of the oven. Line a baking sheet with parchment paper or a silicone baking mat.

Combine the almonds and granulated sugar in a food processor and process until they have the texture of fine meal, scraping the bowl down occasionally to evenly grind the nuts. Transfer the almonds to a bowl and use a spatula to mix in the egg whites, honey, and almond extract until evenly combined.

You can coat the cookies all in confectioners' sugar or a single type of nut, or make an assortment by using several different coatings. Whichever you choose, place each coating in a separate shallow bowl.

Use a tablespoon measure to scoop out level tablespoons of the dough, making thirty-six cookies in total. Roll each dough piece between your palms to form a ball.

To coat the cookies, roll one ball in a topping (confectioners' sugar or nuts), firmly pressing the nuts into the dough with your hands. Continue to coat all the cookies, transferring them to the prepared baking sheet as you form them, allowing 1 inch all around each cookie for spreading.

Bake the cookies until they are light golden and still soft to the touch, 10 to 12 minutes. Transfer the sheet to a wire rack and let the cookies cool completely. Store in an airtight container for up to 2 weeks.

Foglie da Te' pistachio tuiles

I discovered these delightful cookies in Zafferana Etnea, a small town in the foothills of Mount Etna, as I traveled from one pastry shop to the next seeking out unusual local desserts. Curled like a leaf (*foglie* means leaves), the thin wafers are found in every shop in the area, made with almonds, pistachio, or hazelnuts, with each shop claiming the cookie as their own specialty, and the recipe a well-guarded secret. I found an ingredient list on a package of the cookies in one shop and made it my mission to re-create them at home. The wafers are the perfect accompaniment to a scoop of ice cream or a bowl of ricotta mousse, or on their own with a glass of dessert wine. It is impossible to eat just one, or even a few.

Some of the world's best pistachios are grown in Bronte, at the foot of Mount Etna, and the cookies I found in Zafferana were made with thinly sliced pistachios. I suspect these are made using a commercial machine, and I've never seen them sliced this way for sale, either in Italy or in the United States. For the pistachios added at the end, laboriously slice each nut by hand if you must, or blanch the nuts in boiling water for 5 minutes and drain them, which one pastry chef told me makes them very easy to slice. I simply chop them.

The thin cookies are most easily shaped using a template. From a piece of flexible plastic, such as the lid of a pint or quart container, cut all around to remove the outer rim. Bend the plastic in half to make a small cut, then open it and cut out an oval opening measuring about $2^1/2$ by $1^3/4$ inches at the longest and widest points. Now, trim around the opening to leave a $1/2$-inch rim all around.

$1/4$ cup (28 g) raw shelled pistachios

3 tablespoons all-purpose flour

3 tablespoons light brown sugar

1 large egg white

4 tablespoons (57 g) unsalted butter, melted and cooled

$1/2$ teaspoon pure vanilla extract

$1/4$ cup (28 g) chopped or finely slivered raw pistachios

Preheat the oven to 325°F (163°C) with racks in the upper and lower thirds of the oven. Line two baking sheets with a sheet of parchment paper folded in half to make a double thickness.

Combine the whole pistachios, flour, and brown sugar in a food processor (a small capacity one is best for this small quantity) and process until the nuts are ground very fine, like flour. (Alternatively, grind the pistachios and brown sugar in a spice or coffee grinder, using half the nuts and sugar at a time, then transfer them to a bowl and stir in the flour.)

Whisk the egg white until frothy. Stir in the butter until well mixed, then the ground pistachio mixture. Add the vanilla and the chopped pistachios. The mixture will be loose.

Place the cut-out plastic template on one of the prepared baking sheets and drop a teaspoon of the batter into the center. Spread the batter as thinly as possible with the back of a spoon or a small offset spatula to fill the opening. Lift the template and move it to make the next cookie, continuing to form the cookies about 1 inch apart in even rows.

When you have filled both sheets, bake the cookies until they are golden around the edges, about 10 minutes, rotating the pans from front to back and top to bottom halfway through baking. Immediately after removing the baking sheets from the oven, using hot pads and with a long side of one of the baking sheet facing you, gently roll the sheet of parchment with its cookies away from you into a long, tight roll to curl the cookies. Repeat with the second sheet. Let the cookies cool completely on the rolled sheets.

After the cookies have cooled, gently unroll the sheets. Peel off the cookies and transfer them to an airtight container at room temperature for up to 2 weeks.

Biscotti Regina sesame seed cookies

MAKES 60 SMALL COOKIES

Found in pastry shops throughout Palermo, these crunchy cookies are presumed to have been named for Margherita di Savoia, the well-loved second queen (*regina*) of a united Italy. The cookies also go by the name *biscotti reginelle* or, in dialect, *viscuotti 'nciminati*, meaning cookies with sesame. Originally, the cookies were made with *strutto* (lard), but these days butter is more common. In Palermo, they bake them until they are *tostati*—darkly toasted.

The addictive little cookies become even crunchier a day or two after they are baked. Sixty cookies may seem like a lot, but they are wonderful to have on hand for drop-in guests.

2 cups (264 g) all-purpose flour

$^1/_2$ cup (100 g) sugar

1 teaspoon baking powder

$^1/_4$ teaspoon kosher salt

6 tablespoons (85 g) unsalted butter, cut into $^1/_2$-inch cubes

2 large egg yolks

$^1/_4$ cup (60 ml) water

1 teaspoon pure orange extract

Finely grated zest of 1 orange (about 2 teaspoons)

$^1/_2$ cup (120 ml) whole milk

1 cup (194 g) raw (untoasted) sesame seeds

Combine the flour, sugar, baking powder, and salt in a food processor and pulse to mix. Add the butter and process until the mixture looks like coarse meal, stopping and scraping the bowl as needed. Whisk together the egg yolks, water, orange extract, and orange zest in a small bowl. With the processor running, add the egg mixture through the feed tube and continue processing until the dough comes together around the blade. (Alternatively, mix the dough by hand as you would for pie crust.)

Turn the dough out onto a flat surface and knead briefly to make a smooth dough. Wrap the dough in plastic wrap and refrigerate for at least 30 minutes, or up to 1 day. If the dough is very stiff when you are ready to use it, let it stand at room temperature, wrapped, for 20 minutes before proceeding.

Preheat the oven to 400°F (204℃) with a rack in the center of the oven. Line a baking sheet with parchment paper or a silicone baking mat. Put the milk in a bowl and the sesame seeds in a shallow soup bowl.

Divide the dough into six equal pieces. Taking one piece of dough, and keeping the others covered, roll with your hands on a lightly floured surface to form a rope about $^1/_2$ inch thick. Use a knife or pastry cutter to cut the dough into ten segments, each about $1^1/_2$ inches long. Roll each piece of dough briefly between your palms to form a football shape with slightly tapered ends. Drop the cookies into the milk as you form them.

To keep things from getting messy, use one hand to transfer the cookies from the milk to the sesame seeds, and the other hand to press each cookie into the seeds until it is completely coated on all sides and slightly flattened. Transfer the cookies to the prepared sheet as you form them. Continue with the remaining dough to make five long rows of twelve cookies each on the baking sheet. They will be quite close but should not be touching.

Bake until the cookies are firm and the seeds are well toasted, about 25 minutes. Transfer the baking sheet to a rack until the cookies are completely cool.

Store the cooled cookies in an airtight container at room temperature for up to 2 weeks, or freeze for up to a month; thaw for several hours in the closed container at room temperature.

Biscotti Eureka almond-filled spiral cookies

I discovered these pretty almond-filled spiral cookies while wandering through Ortigia, in Siracusa, in the window of Caffe Pasticceria Marciante. Intrigued by the name, I went inside to inquire about them. The clerk told me the shop had created the cookie 15 years earlier in honor of Archimedes, the famous Syracuse-born inventor, engineer, and mathematician. The cookie is formed in the shape of Archimedes' spiral and is called "eureka" to recall his exclamation at the discovery of volume displacement: that the volume of a solid can be measured by the amount of liquid it displaces. (In lay terms, you could measure the volume of a chestnut by the amount of water that spilled out of your full glass when you dropped it in.) On making his discovery, Archimedes is said to have run through Siracusa's streets naked, yelling, "Eureka!"—Greek for "I have found it!"—so excited by this newfound knowledge that he'd forgotten to dress.

I don't know whether I enjoy the story or the cookie more, but I was delighted by the cookie's spiral shape and Sicilian almonds, Tarocco blood oranges, orange blossom honey, and candied orange peel.

PASTRY

1^1/$_2$ cups (200 g) all-purpose flour

Pinch of kosher salt

7 tablespoons (100 g) unsalted butter, cut into ^{1}/$_2$-inch cubes

About ^{1}/$_4$ cup (60 ml) ice water

FILLING

1 cup (150 g) blanched almonds (page 189)

6 tablespoons (75 g) sugar

1 large egg white

^{1}/$_3$ cup (100 g) blood orange marmalade (page 194) or orange marmalade

1 tablespoon orange blossom honey

^{1}/$_4$ cup packed (50 g) minced candied orange peel (page 193)

1 egg white, lightly beaten, for brushing

^{1}/$_2$ cup (67 g) finely chopped blanched almonds (page 189), for coating

To make the pastry, combine the flour and salt in a food processor and briefly pulse. Add the butter and pulse until it is in small crumbs. With the machine running, add the ice water through the feed tube just until the mixture comes together around the blade. When you stop the processor and pinch some of the mixture between your fingers, the pastry should easily hold together. If it does not, pulse in more water, a teaspoon at a time, until it can be pinched together.

Press the pastry into a 6- by 3-inch rectangle, wrap tightly in plastic wrap, and refrigerate for at least 1 hour, or up to 3 days, before rolling.

To make the filling, process the almonds with the sugar in a food processor to make a fine meal. Add the egg white, marmalade, and honey, and process until thoroughly combined. Remove the bowl from the processor and use a spatula to fold in the orange peel.

To form the cookies, roll the pastry on lightly floured parchment paper to form a large rectangle about ^{1}/$_4$-inch thick. Trim the edges to make a 16- by 9-inch rectangle.

Spread the filling evenly over the rectangle, leaving about ^{1}/$_2$ inch uncovered around the edges. With a long edge of the pastry facing you and beginning at that edge, work slowly across the entire width of the dough, rolling it toward the opposite edge to form a tight log. Place the log seam side down on the parchment paper and slide the

CONTINUED

log and parchment paper onto a rimless baking sheet. Refrigerate until firm, at least 1 hour or up to 1 day.

To bake the cookies, preheat the oven to 350°F (177°C) with a rack in the center of the oven.

Slide the log onto a flat surface, leaving the parchment paper on the baking sheet. Brush the top and sides of the log with the egg white and press the chopped almonds evenly over the surface. Rotate the log to brush the bottom with egg white and coat it with almonds. Cut the log into $7/8$-inch-thick slices, placing them cut side down on the parchment paper–lined baking sheet, spacing them 1 inch apart.

Bake until the cookies are golden, about 30 minutes. Cool completely on the baking sheet or on a wire rack before serving or storing in an airtight container for up to 7 days. Freeze the tightly wrapped cookies for longer storage.

Africano chocolate-hazelnut cake rolls

I first learned of this exceptional dessert while honeymooning in Palermo, my first trip with my husband to his native city. Lino was excited to share all his favorite foods with me, including the sweets he grew up with. When he ordered "*un Africano*" in a pastry shop, I was intrigued; I'd heard the term used to refer to dark-skinned people of any heritage, but never to a dessert. What came to the table was a rich cake roll filled with chocolate-hazelnut paste, then enrobed in dark chocolate, the ends dipped in white chocolate and chopped pistachios. When I began writing this book, I knew I had to include the Africano—after all, it remains one of my husband's favorites, and, to my knowledge, there is no written account of how to make it. When my sister-in-law Giuseppina, who lives in Palermo, recently visited, we got to work re-creating the pastry. I think ours are even nicer than the ones in the pastry shops, where they are found only during the cool months, kept on top of the counter. Indeed, their texture is best when they are cool but not ice cold. Now I make them at any time of year, refrigerating them, and letting them stand for a few minutes at room temperature before digging in, if I can wait that long.

Even if you love dark chocolate, as I do, for the best consistency in the filling, avoid using chocolate with over 55 percent cacao.

FILLING

- 9 ounces (255 g) semisweet chocolate (40 to 55 percent cacao)
- 1 cup (240 g) hazelnut paste, homemade (page 192) or store-bought
- 1 cup (125 g) confectioners' sugar

CAKE

- 3 large eggs
- 3 tablespoons granulated sugar
- 2 teaspoons mild-flavored honey, such as clover or orange blossom
- ¹/₃ cup plus 1 tablespoon (50 g) cake flour

To make the filling, melt the chocolate in a metal bowl set over but not touching simmering water in a saucepan, just until you can stir the chocolate smooth. Remove the bowl from the heat and cool to 88°F (31°C), or until it feels neither warm nor cool when you touch a drop against your lip. Stir in the hazelnut paste until evenly combined. Sift in the confectioners' sugar, mixing to completely incorporate it. Let the filling stand, uncovered, until it is thick and spreadable, like a thick nut paste, while you make the cake.

To make the cake, preheat the oven to 350°F (177°C) with a rack in the center of the oven. Line an 11- by 17-inch rimmed baking sheet with parchment paper; butter and flour the parchment paper.

Beat the eggs, sugar, and honey in a stand mixer with the whisk attachment for 15 minutes, beginning at medium speed and increasing to high after the ingredients are blended. Sift the flour over the top, about one-third at a time, gently folding after each addition with a large spatula to completely incorporate the flour without deflating the eggs more than necessary.

Use a small offset spatula to spread the batter in an even layer over the prepared pan. Bake until light golden all over, 8 to 10 minutes. Lift out the cake on its parchment paper and transfer it to a flat surface

INGREDIENTS AND METHOD CONTINUED

COATING

16 ounces (454 g) dark chocolate (55 to 60 percent cacao)

3 tablespoons safflower or other neutral-tasting vegetable oil

6 ounces (170 g) white chocolate

1/2 cup (75 g) finely chopped raw pistachios

with a long side facing you. Trim away the crusty edges on all sides of the cake, then cut the cake into four equal sections, about 4 inches wide, marking the cake on both sides and using a straight edge to cut it evenly. Turn the cake pieces bottom side up.

Check the filling: If it is thin, stir briefly over a bowl of ice water, taking care not to slosh water into the bowl, until it is thick and spreadable, like peanut butter. While the cake is still slightly warm and pliable, divide the filling evenly among the four cake pieces, then spread it evenly over the surface of each piece. With a long side facing you, roll one filled cake tightly away from you into a long roll. Continue to roll the remaining three pieces.

Transfer the rolls, seam side down, to a baking sheet lined with plastic wrap and refrigerate for at least 15 minutes to firm the filling. Trim the ends from the rolls to neaten them, then cut each roll into three equal segments. Return the individual rolls to the lined baking sheet, seam side down.

To make the coating, melt the dark chocolate with 2 tablespoons of the oil in a bowl set over, but not touching, simmering water in a saucepan until the chocolate is melted and smooth. Remove the saucepan from the heat, keeping the chocolate over the hot water to maintain the right consistency for dipping. Dip one of the rolls into the melted chocolate, holding it from one end and then the other to completely cover it, then hold it over the bowl to let the excess chocolate run back into the bowl. Return the roll to the lined baking sheet. Continue to coat all of the rolls. Refrigerate until set, at least 30 minutes.

Line a second baking sheet with plastic wrap. Melt the white chocolate with the remaining 1 tablespoon of oil in a bowl over, but not touching, simmering water. Put the pistachios in a small bowl. If you have them, put on disposable latex gloves to keep from leaving fingerprints on the rolls. Dip one end of a roll into the white chocolate, then into the chopped pistachios; repeat to coat the other end. Transfer the roll to the newly lined baking sheet. Continue to dip the remaining rolls. Refrigerate until set, 15 to 30 minutes, before serving.

Refrigerate leftover *Africani* in a single layer in an airtight container for up to 1 week.

Crostata al Gelo di Mellone
watermelon pudding tart

This recipe dresses up refreshing watermelon *gelo* as the filling for a lattice-topped tart. The chocolate chips simulate the watermelon's black seeds and add a contrasting crunch to the smooth *gelo*.

You will need to prepare the short-crust pastry several hours in advance. After the dough has chilled, prepare the *gelo* up to the point of cooking it, roll out the dough and fit it into the pan, then cook the *gelo* so that you can pour it warm into the crust before it begins to firm up.

Short-crust pastry (page 183, double crust)

Gelo di Mellone (page 60), still warm

2 tablespoons semisweet or dark mini chocolate chips or chopped chocolate

2 tablespoons chopped raw pistachios, for garnish

Confectioners' sugar, for garnish

Make the pastry and divide the dough into two pieces, one slightly larger than the other. Flatten the pieces into disks, wrap in plastic wrap, and chill for several hours.

Preheat the oven to 350°F (177°C) with a rack in the center of the oven. Butter a 10-inch fluted tart pan with a removable bottom, or a 10-inch springform pan.

Leaving the smaller disk of pastry dough in the refrigerator, roll the larger disk between two sheets of plastic wrap to make a 13-inch round. Remove the plastic from one side and invert the dough over the prepared pan, nestling it evenly into the bottom and sides. In the springform, it should come about $1^1/2$ inches up the sides; in the tart pan it will slightly overhang the edges. Refrigerate the crust-lined pan while you roll the second disk between two sheets of plastic wrap to make a $10^1/2$-inch round. Use a fluted cutter to cut the dough into $3/4$-inch strips, making at least ten strips. Slide the dough onto a rimless baking sheet and refrigerate until you are ready to use it.

Pour the warm *gelo* into the pastry-lined pan. Sprinkle the chocolate chips or chopped chocolate evenly over the top. Place the strips of pastry over the top, spacing five strips evenly in one direction, then laying the remaining five strips at about a 45-degree angle over the top, without weaving, to form a diamond pattern. Using the fluted cutter, trim the dough around the edges to about $1/2$ inch above the filling. Fold the excess bottom dough over the strips, pressing the strips and bottom dough together to seal them.

Bake until the *crostata* is golden, 40 to 45 minutes. Cool completely in the pan on the rack, then remove the pan sides. Refrigerate until very cold, at least 6 hours.

To serve, sprinkle the top with the chopped pistachios and dust with confectioners' sugar. Cut with a sharp knife into wedges. Serve cold.

Cassata Siciliana decorated ricotta-filled sponge cake

This ornate cake is among the prettiest found in Palermo's pastry shops. A must for Easter, the ricotta-filled cake decorated with marzipan, iced, and crowned with large pieces of candied fruit is found on pastry shop shelves year round. If Cassata al Forno (page 47) is the country bumpkin made at home throughout the year, the Cassata Siciliana is its sophisticated city cousin, more often on order from a *pasticceria*. In Palermo, the cake is covered with a pourable fondant that home cooks would purchase already made, but after experimenting I found that the simple glaze I developed for the Sospiri (page 129) works very well, remaining soft after it sets, as it should for this dessert. I also use my homemade almond paste in place of the typical marzipan; it's less sweet and has the right texture.

The traditional springtime fruit decorations include ribbons of the candied squash called *zuccata,* shaped as flower petals with pieces of candied pear or orange slices between the folds and a candied mandarin orange in the center. Between the petals might be *cedro candito* (candied citron), candied orange, candied pears dyed green or red, or other candied fruits. You can candy your own fruits following my instructions for candied orange peel (page 193), or use whatever good-quality candied fruits you have available. For the ornate finish found in pastry shops and shown here, pipe on swirls and dots of royal icing.

You'll want to get started a couple of days before you will serve this masterpiece. The ricotta cream filling must be prepared a day before assembling the cassata. You can also make the sponge cake a day ahead of assembly if you wish; cover the cake layers in their pans with plastic wrap and store at room temperature. The assembled *cassata* will then need an additional day to allow the cake to soak up the flavors layered within.

RICOTTA FILLING

3 cups (681 g) fresh ricotta (page 186), well drained

1 cup (200 g) granulated sugar

^{1}/$_4$ cup (42 g) semisweet or dark mini chocolate chips or chopped chocolate

2 (9-inch) sponge cakes (page 184, double recipe)

SIMPLE SYRUP

^{1}/$_4$ cup (50 g) granulated sugar

^{1}/$_2$ cup (120 ml) water

^{1}/$_4$ cup (60 ml) maraschino liqueur, such as Luxardo

Prepare the ricotta filling the day before assembling the cake. Press the ricotta through an ultrafine-mesh strainer or splatter screen (see page 14) into a large bowl. Add the granulated sugar and mix well. Cover and refrigerate overnight. (Wait until indicated to add the chocolate chips.)

To prepare the cake layers, remove them from the pans and trim away the dark edges all around the cakes. Use a serrated knife in a sawing motion to level the tops, then invert the layers and trim the thin dark layer from the cake bottoms. Cut each cake horizontally into two even layers. Set aside.

To make the simple syrup, stir the granulated sugar with the water in a small saucepan over low heat to completely dissolve the sugar. Remove from the heat and let cool, then stir in the maraschino liqueur. Set aside.

INGREDIENTS AND METHOD CONTINUED

ALMOND PASTE

¹/₂ cup plus 2 tablespoons
(200 g / 7 ounces) almond
paste, homemade (page
192) or store-bought

Green food coloring, such as
AmeriColor Avocado #129

GLAZE

2 cups (250 g) confectioners'
sugar

¹/₄ cup hot water, plus more
if needed

2 tablespoons corn syrup or
glucose syrup

Assorted candied fruits, for
garnish

To color the almond paste, put the paste on a flat surface such as a plastic cutting board. (You may want to line the board with plastic wrap to avoid stains.) Pinch off a knob (about a 1-inch ball) and knead in 2 drops of the food coloring to thoroughly distribute the color. You will use this deeply colored piece to calibrate the color in the rest of the almond paste. Take a small piece of the colored almond paste and knead it thoroughly into the remaining (uncolored) paste until it is evenly colored throughout. Continue kneading in the deeply colored almond paste until you are satisfied with the color. (A light to medium green is typical.) To darken it further, repeat the process: Pinch off and color a small piece, then knead it bit by bit into the rest of the almond paste to obtain an even color. If the almond paste is too dry to work with, moisten your hands to aid in kneading it. Once you are satisfied with the color, roll out the almond paste between two pieces of plastic wrap to a rectangle of at least 2 inches wide and 16 inches long, and about ¹/₈ inch thick. Set aside.

To assemble the *cassata*, line a 9- by 2-inch cassata pan or pie pan with plastic wrap. Cut two of the four cake layers all around into trapezoidal shapes that are 2¹/₄ inches at the base and 1¹/₂ inches at the top, cutting just 2 inches into the cake toward the center to leave behind a round about 5 inches across. You will need about fourteen trapezoids, or enough to fit all around the pan. (Be sure to use an even number.) Fit seven of the cake pieces along the sides of the pan with the large ends facing down fitting the bases close together.

Using one of the trapezoidal cake pieces as a guide, cut the rolled almond paste into seven trapezoidal pieces. (You may not need all the almond paste.) Place the almond paste pieces small side down between the cake pieces, fitting the pieces snugly together to completely cover the sides of the pan. Place the remaining seven cake pieces small side down to cover the almond paste pieces to make a solid cake layer over the sides of the pan.

Cut a round from one of the remaining cake layers to fit the bottom of the pan, with the cake snuggled tightly against the cake pieces lining the sides. Place in the pan, then brush all of the exposed cake on the bottom and sides of the pan with about half of the simple syrup to soak it well. Stir the chocolate chips into the ricotta cream, then spread the filling over the cake. Place the remaining cake layer over the top and press firmly to fully enclose the filling, patching up any gaps around the edge with scraps of sponge cake. Brush the remaining simple syrup over the top.

Cover the cake with plastic wrap, then top with a large plate and place a weight on top, such as a large can of tomatoes. Refrigerate overnight.

To make the glaze, whisk together the confectioners' sugar, hot water, and corn syrup in a heatproof bowl. Place the bowl over a small pan of simmering water so that the bowl is over but not touching the water. Stir the glaze just until it is smooth and warm, about 1 minute. Remove the pan from the heat, leaving the bowl of glaze over the water to keep it warm. The consistency of the glaze should allow you to lightly coat the cassata, with the green almond paste visible through the glaze. If it is too thick, stir hot water into the glaze a teaspoon at a time to obtain the right consistency.

To glaze the *cassata*, remove the weight, plate, and top plastic wrap from the cake. Invert the cassata onto a flat serving plate. Remove the pan, then carefully peel away the plastic wrap. Spread the glaze with a small offset spatula evenly all over the cake to form a thin coating. If it becomes too thick to spread, add a teaspoon or two of hot water to keep it spreadable. Carefully scrape away any excess glaze that has pooled onto the serving plate, then refrigerate the *cassata* to set the glaze, at least 4 hours or up to one day.

To decorate the *cassata*, place candied fruits on top of the cake in a decorative pattern. (This is the time to pipe on royal icing, if you wish.) Serve the *cassata* cold, cut into wedges. Cover and refrigerate leftovers for up to 4 days.

Torta Gattopardo ricotta and pistachio mousse cake

SERVES 12 TO 16 | GLUTEN FREE

This cake takes its name from the 1958 novel *Il Gattopardo* (*The Leopard*) by Giuseppe Tomasi di Lampedusa. Depicting Sicilian life in the 1880s, the novel became an Italian bestseller, and in 1963, was made into a film. Both the film and novel brought a picture of *la vita Siciliana* to the rest of Italy and the world, inspiring many Italian chefs to name dishes, both savory and sweet, for *Il Gattopardo.*

My sister-in-law Giuseppina developed this cake, though I have replaced her pistachio cookie layers with crisp-tender pistachio dacquoise and glazed the cake in white chocolate rather than dark for a pretty finish. The cake's several steps require some advance planning, but it is well worth the effort and is perfect for a special occasion. To make the cake ahead, freeze the filled but unglazed cake until you are ready to glaze and serve it.

Gelatin sheets are easily found in baking supply stores or online and are much more reliable than powdered gelatin (see page 17). While you are at the baking supply store, look for clear acetate cake wrap sheets to give your cake a professionally finished look. To make a pistachio-toned glaze revealing the flavor of the filling, the best color I've found is AmeriColor Avocado #129 (see Sources, page 203). The white chocolate glaze is pretty without color as well.

RICOTTA MOUSSE

3 cups (681 g) well-drained ricotta

1 cup (200 g) granulated sugar

1 cup (240 ml) plus 2 tablespoons heavy cream

3 sheets silver grade gelatin

PISTACHIO DACQUOISE

1 cup (133 g) raw shelled pistachios

3/4 cup plus 1 tablespoon (100 g) confectioners' sugar

4 large egg whites

3 tablespoons granulated sugar

PISTACHIO MOUSSE

2 sheets silver grade gelatin

1 1/8 cups (320 g) freshly made (hot) pastry cream (page 185)

1/3 cup (74 g) pistachio paste (page 190)

3/4 cup (180 ml) heavy cream

1 tablespoon granulated sugar

To make the ricotta mousse, press the ricotta through an ultrafine-mesh strainer or splatter screen (see page 14) into a bowl. Use a spatula to stir in the granulated sugar.

In a separate bowl, whip 1 cup of the cream using an electric mixer until firm peaks form. Use a large spatula to fold the whipped cream into the ricotta mixture; set aside.

Put the gelatin into a small bowl of cool water to completely submerge it; let stand 5 minutes to soften. In a bowl in the microwave or in a small saucepan over medium heat, heat the remaining 2 tablespoons of cream until it simmers. Squeeze the water from the soaked gelatin and stir it into the hot cream until it dissolves completely. Stir 1/4 cup of the ricotta mixture into the dissolved gelatin, then use a large spatula to fold this mixture back into the ricotta mixture until well mixed. Cover the mousse and refrigerate for 2 hours.

To make the dacquoise layers, preheat the oven to 350°F (177°C) with the racks in the upper and lower thirds of the oven. Line two baking sheets with parchment paper. Using the outer ring of a 9-inch springform pan as a guide, draw a circle in pencil on each piece of parchment paper, then turn over the parchment paper so that the writing can be seen through the paper. Lightly oil the parchment paper with neutral-tasting oil within and slightly beyond the two circles.

WHITE CHOCOLATE GLAZE

2 sheets silver grade gelatin

³/₄ cup (180 ml) heavy cream

9 ounces (255 g) white chocolate, chopped

A few drops of green food coloring (optional)

³/₄ cup (100 g) raw shelled pistachios, chopped medium-fine, for sides of cake

Combine the pistachios and confectioners' sugar in a blender and process until the nuts are the texture of medium-fine cornmeal, scraping down the bowl as needed.

Beat the egg whites at medium speed in a stand mixer fitted with the whisk attachment until they form soft peaks. With the mixer running, add the granulated sugar in a few additions, then increase the speed to high and beat until firm peaks form that are not at all dry. (Alternatively, use a handheld electric mixer.) Use a large spatula to fold in the pistachio mixture in three additions, until it is fully incorporated.

Pipe or spread the pistachio mixture to fill the two circles, dividing it equally between the two sheets. Use a small offset spatula to spread the batter to the edge of the circles in an even layer.

Bake the layers, rotating the pans top to bottom and front to back halfway through baking, until they are dry to the touch and light golden all over, 25 to 30 minutes. Transfer the layers on their parchment paper liners to a flat surface. The cakes will have expanded slightly: To ensure they will fit into the pan, trim all around the edges of the warm layers with a sharp paring knife, using a 9-inch cake pan as a guide. Slide the layers onto a wire rack to cool completely.

To make the pistachio mousse, put the gelatin into a small bowl of cool water to completely submerge it; let stand 5 minutes to soften. Squeeze the water from the soaked gelatin and stir it into the hot pastry cream until it dissolves completely. Stir in the pistachio paste until well mixed. Refrigerate or let stand at room temperature until cool.

Whip the cream with the granulated sugar using an electric mixer until firm peaks form. Whisk the cooled pistachio mixture to loosen it, then use a large spatula to fold in the whipped cream.

To assemble the cake, line the sides of a 9-inch springform pan with an acetate sheet (see headnote), if using. Place one of the cakes top side up in the bottom of the pan. Spread half of the ricotta mousse evenly over the cake. Set the second cake layer top side up over the cream, pressing it gently to evenly settle the mousse.

CONTINUED

Spread all of the pistachio mousse evenly over the top. Freeze, uncovered, until the pistachio mousse is firm, about 1 hour.

Spread the remaining ricotta mousse over the top, then drag a straight edge—such as the back of a long knife—across the top to perfectly level it. Freeze, uncovered, until firm, at least 4 hours or overnight.

To make the glaze, put the gelatin into a small bowl of cool water to completely submerge it; let stand 5 minutes to soften. Bring the cream to a boil in a medium saucepan. Off the heat, add the white chocolate, wait 1 minute, then stir with a whisk until the mixture is smooth. Squeeze the water from the soaked gelatin and stir it into the chocolate mixture until it dissolves completely. If you are using it, stir in the food coloring, a drop or two at a time, until the glaze is a light pistachio green color. Set aside to cool slightly while you prepare the cake for glazing.

To finish the cake, remove the outer ring from the springform pan and peel off the acetate liner if you used one. Leaving the cake on its base, or carefully transferring it to a 9-inch cardboard cake circle, set the cake on a wire rack set over a rimmed baking sheet to catch the dripping chocolate. Check the glaze; it should be slightly thickened and lukewarm to the touch (about 90°F/32°C). Pour the glaze over the frozen cake, starting in the center, then pouring it around the edges to fully coat the top and sides of the cake.

Press the chopped pistachios onto the cake sides to cover them. Refrigerate the cake for several hours or overnight to thaw, allowing the frozen cake to become soft and mousse-like before serving.

To serve, dip a sharp knife into warm water and wipe dry before cutting the cake into wedges.

Torta di Pistacchio pistachio cake

SERVES 8 | GLUTEN FREE

Other than the substitution of pistachios, this recipe is nearly identical to the flourless walnut cake in my first book, *My Calabria*. I tasted many pistachio cakes while traveling through Sicily, but this simple, light cake with intense pistachio flavor remains my favorite. For a splurge, cut the cake into two layers and spread a jar of *crema di pistacchio* imported from Bronte, Sicily, between them.

1²/₃ cups (225 g) raw shelled pistachios

6 large eggs, separated, at room temperature

Pinch of kosher salt

³/₄ cup (150 g) granulated sugar

Finely grated zest of 1 lemon

Confectioners' sugar, for dusting

Preheat the oven to 325°F (163°C) with a rack in the center of the oven. Butter the bottom and sides of a 9-inch springform pan with at least 2³/₄-inch-high sides.

Process the pistachios in a food processor in two batches until they are the texture of fine cornmeal, with only a few slightly larger pieces. Set aside.

Using a stand mixer fitted with the whisk attachment, beat the egg whites and salt at low speed to break them up, then raise the speed to medium and beat until they hold soft peaks. Increase the speed to medium-high and gradually add 6 tablespoons (75 g) of the granulated sugar, then continue to beat until medium-firm peaks form that are not at all dry. (Alternatively, use a handheld mixer.) Set aside.

In a separate bowl, beat the yolks with the remaining 6 tablespoons (75 g) granulated sugar at medium speed until they are thick and pale, about 4 minutes. Mix in the lemon zest. Use a large spatula to fold the egg yolk mixture gently into the whites. Gently fold in the ground pistachios in three additions, folding each time just until the nuts are incorporated.

Spread the batter evenly in the prepared pan. Bake until the cake is golden and firm to the touch and pulls away from the sides of the pan, about 40 minutes. A toothpick inserted near the center should come out clean. Cool the cake in the pan on a wire rack for 20 minutes, then remove the sides of the pan and let cool completely.

Transfer the cooled cake on its base to a serving platter, or carefully run a metal spatula under the cake and slide it directly onto the platter. Just before serving, sift confectioners' sugar over the surface. Cut with a serrated or thin, sharp knife.

Cassata al Forno baked ricotta tart

In Palermo, you will find two traditional styles of *cassata*—the elegant Cassata Siciliana (page 39), prepared for Easter and decorated with marzipan and candied fruit, and its rustic cousin, the Cassata al Forno. Both use the same ricotta filling, but in the *al forno* version, the filling is baked in a pastry crust and served upside down.

This recipe requires some advance planning because the filling must be made a day before the *cassata* is filled and baked, and then the finished *cassata* needs several hours or overnight to chill and set before serving.

3 cups (680 g) fresh ricotta (page 186), well drained

1 1/4 cups (250 g) granulated sugar

2 teaspoons pure vanilla extract

Short-crust pastry (page 183, double crust)

1/4 cup (42 g) semisweet or dark mini chocolate chips or chopped chocolate

Confectioners' sugar, for dusting

Make the ricotta filling the night before you will assemble the cassata. Use a flat-edge pastry scraper or spatula to press the ricotta through an ultrafine-mesh strainer or splatter screen (see page 14) into a large bowl. Stir in the granulated sugar and vanilla. Cover and refrigerate overnight.

Divide the short-crust pastry into two pieces, one slightly larger than the other. Flatten into disks, wrap in plastic wrap, and chill for at least 1 hour.

When you are ready to assemble the *cassata*, preheat the oven to 425°F (218°C) with a rack in the center of the oven. Butter and flour a 9- by 2-inch cake or pie pan, knocking out any excess flour.

Roll the larger disk of pastry dough with a rolling pin between two sheets of plastic wrap to form a 13-inch round. Remove one piece of plastic wrap, then invert the pastry over the pan, centering it, and pressing it into place using the plastic wrap as an aid. Peel away the plastic and patch any small tears. Trim the dough flush against the top of the pan. Refrigerate while you roll the second dough round.

Roll the second dough disk between two pieces of plastic wrap into a round just a shade under 9 inches; slide with the plastic wrap onto a baking sheet and refrigerate until needed.

Stir the chocolate pieces into the ricotta filling, then spread the mixture evenly in the dough-lined pan. Peel off the plastic wrap from the top of the 9-inch dough round and flip the dough, centering it over the filling. Remove the second sheet of plastic wrap. Press the dough slightly into the filling, then press and pinch the top and bottom dough together to form a tight seal.

CONTINUED

Bake the *cassata* until it is golden, about 30 minutes. Let it cool completely in the pan on a wire rack, at least 3 hours. Run a knife around the edge of the pan, then invert the *cassata* onto a flat plate but do not remove the pan; refrigerate overnight to set the filling.

To serve, remove the pan and dust the *cassata* with confectioners' sugar. Cut the cassata into wedges with a sharp knife.

Cuccia di Santa Lucia wheat berry pudding for the feast of Saint Lucia

In Palermo, December 13 marks the Festa di Santa Lucia, when this dessert is eaten to recall a time when the people prayed to Saint Lucia for food to nourish the masses. As the legend goes, when a ship showed up in the harbor carrying wheat, the starving people could not take the time to grind and bake it into bread. Instead, they cooked the wheat into this pudding. Since that day, Sicilians have showed their gratitude by eating wheat prepared only in this way during the holiday—no breads or other products made with ground wheat are eaten on December 13. There's no reason to wait for the Festa di Santa Lucia to make this simple and satisfying dessert— and while the Sicilians might disagree, I think it's terrific for breakfast as well.

The towns and families of Sicily each seem to have their own version of this pudding, and other variations are found throughout Southern Italy. In Calabria, the wheat berries are dressed with *mosto cotto* and nuts. In Sicily, the wheat berries might be cooked in milk, with or without cinnamon, and topped with chocolate, candied fruit, or the candied squash known as *zuccata*. This version comes from my husband Lino's family, still living in Palermo.

Use hulled berries, the ones with the outer layer removed, often found in the bulk foods section of health food stores. Plan ahead: the berries must be soaked for three days in advance. Alternatively, substitute *farro perlato* (pearled farro) and omit the soaking.

1 cup (200 g) hulled wheat berries

6 cups (1.4 L) water, plus more as needed

1 teaspoon kosher salt

3 cups (681 g) fresh ricotta (page 186), well drained

3/4 cup (150 g) sugar

1/3 cup (57 g) semisweet or dark chocolate chips

Ground cinnamon, for garnish (optional)

Finely chopped raw pistachios, for garnish

Place the wheat berries in a bowl and cover with 4 cups of cold water. Cover and set aside at room temperature for 3 days, draining off and replacing the water once a day.

Drain the wheat berries and transfer them to a 4-quart saucepan. Add the water and salt. Bring to a boil, then adjust the heat to cook the berries at a gentle boil until they are tender and most of them have split, about 90 minutes, adding water if needed to keep the wheat berries covered by about an inch.

Remove the pan from the heat and let the wheat berries cool completely in the water. Drain the cooled wheat berries and set them aside.

Press the ricotta through an ultrafine-mesh strainer or splatter screen (see page 14) into a bowl. Stir together the ricotta and sugar in a mixing bowl. Stir in the chocolate chips and the reserved wheat berries until they are evenly coated. Transfer to a large serving bowl or spoon into individual dessert cups, using about 1/2 cup per serving. Sprinkle the tops with cinnamon, if desired, and top with the chopped pistachios.

Refrigerate leftovers in an airtight container for up to 4 days.

Cannoli Siciliani Sicilian cannoli

Cannoli are found all over Sicily, but my favorite are the ones found in and around Palermo. As with many Italian dishes, there is much debate about the dessert's origin, with most lore focused on Carnevale and the sweet treats created in convents. The name *cannolo* (singular of cannoli) is likely derived from the Italian word *canne,* the giant bamboo, *Arundo donax,* which grows wild all over Italy. Separated by joints about every 8 inches, the reeds make perfect forms for frying the shells. I still use my traditional *canne* forms, but the forms made from tin or stainless steel you are likely to find at your local cookware store work equally well. (See Sources, page 203.)

You will find cannoli variations all over Sicily, with most of the differences in the filling. Across the island, you will find it with cinnamon or various candied fruits in the filling. There are also variations in the decoration of the finished cannoli: they might come with candied orange peel in Palermo, or the ends might be studded with a cherry or dipped in chopped chocolate or the local pistachios in Bronte. The simplest filling—and my favorite—is the one found in Palermo.

The crispy, blistered shells are created with the addition of either vinegar or Marsala wine to the cannoli dough—sometimes both. The recipe comes from a cousin of my mother-in-law, who worked at Caflisch, Palermo's original Swiss pastry shop, in the 1950s and '60s. I've substituted butter for the *strutto* (lard) and made some minor adjustments to produce cannoli that are even better than the ones I remember in Sicily. Using a pasta machine is the best way to roll the dough. The dough may be made ahead and frozen, well wrapped in plastic wrap, for up to 3 months; thaw overnight in the refrigerator before rolling.

For tips on making great cannoli, see page 56.

CANNOLI SHELLS

- 1³/₄ cups (231 g) all-purpose flour
- 1 tablespoon granulated sugar
- 2 teaspoons unsweetened Dutch-processed cocoa powder
- ¹/₄ cup (60 ml) red wine vinegar
- 3 tablespoons (45 ml) Marsala wine, plus a few drops more, if needed
- 2 tablespoons unsalted butter, melted and cooled
- 1 large egg white, lightly beaten, for sealing the shells
- Safflower or other neutral-tasting vegetable oil, for frying

To make the shells, stir together the flour, granulated sugar, and cocoa in a bowl. Make a well in the center and add the vinegar, Marsala, and melted butter. Begin mixing with a fork to combine, then continue mixing with your hands to form a shaggy dough. Knead for a minute or two to allow the dough to absorb all of the flour. The dough will be stiff, but if it is too difficult to handle, add a few additional drops of Marsala to bring the dough together.

Knead the dough on a flat surface for several minutes, pressing it away with the heel of your hand, until it is nearly smooth. It should have the texture of pasta dough. Wrap the dough in plastic wrap and refrigerate for at least 1 hour, or up to 2 days.

Divide the dough into four pieces and flatten one piece with the palm of your hand. (Keep the remaining dough covered with plastic.) Roll the dough piece using a pasta machine: Run it through at the widest setting, fold the sheet in half, and roll again at the same setting. Adjust the machine to the next narrower setting and repeat. Continue rolling and

INGREDIENTS AND METHOD CONTINUED

Cannoli Siciliani, *continued*

FILLING

4 cups (907 g) fresh ricotta (page 186), well drained

1 cup (200 g) granulated sugar

1 teaspoon pure vanilla extract

1/2 cup (85 g) semisweet or dark mini chocolate chips or chopped chocolate

Confectioners' sugar, to finish

Strips of candied orange peel, about 2 by 1/4 inches (page 193; optional)

adjusting the machine until the dough is 1/16 inch thick and about 2 feet long by 4 to 5 inches wide. (Alternatively, roll the dough on a flat surface using a rolling pin to make a large round about 1/16 inch thick. You may need to let the dough rest periodically, as it is very elastic.) Cover the dough sheet with plastic wrap and continue rolling the remaining three dough balls, one at a time, until they have all been rolled.

Heat 2 inches of oil in a large, heavy pot (about 8 inches in diameter and 4 inches deep) over medium heat until it reaches 350°F (117°C). Line a baking sheet with paper towels.

While the oil heats, cut all of the rolled dough pieces into ovals that are approximately 5 by 4 inches (see tips, page 56). Reroll the remaining dough to form additional cannoli shells.

Center a cannoli form over one of the dough ovals running the long way. Wrap one short end up and over the form, pressing it lightly onto the form. Dab the dough lightly with egg white, then wrap the other short end over it, overlapping the two by about 3/4 inch, pressing them firmly together. Other than where the dough overlaps, let the dough hang loose rather than pressing it onto the form.

Fry the shells, still wrapped around the forms, one at a time, taking care not to splash the oil as you gently slide them in. As it sits in the oil, turn the shell constantly with tongs for even cooking. After about 30 seconds, use tongs to carefully slide the shell off of

CANNOLI LORE

Cannoli are strongly associated with Sicily throughout the world, in part thanks to the movie *The Godfather*. There are many legends about the pastry's origin: Some say it started as a convent sweet, others that is named for the reed used as a form for frying the dough. Still others, noting that *cannolo* is the Italian word for faucet, suggest that the name is meant as a Carnevale-style pun: open the tap and out pours the ricotta filling.

The town of Piana degli Albanesi in the province of Palermo—named for the Albanians who have lived there for generations—holds what is perhaps Italy's largest cannoli festival each spring, the Sagra del Cannolo. Included in the *festa* are all manner of meetings, workshops, conferences, debates, and, of course, tastings—including the march of the giant cannolo—all focused on this ricotta-filled sweet.

the form (set the form aside to cool), then use the tongs to gently and completely submerge the shell, allowing the inside to cook. The shell is ready when its surface is blistered, and it is a shade or two darker than when you began, but not dark brown, about 60 to 90 seconds altogether. Allow the oil to drip back into the pot before transferring the shell to the baking sheet lined with paper towels to drain and cool. Fry the remaining shells in the same manner, allowing the forms to cool before reusing them.

Let the cannoli shells cool completely before filling them.

To make the filling, press the ricotta through an ultrafine-mesh strainer or splatter screen (see page 14) into a large bowl. Use a spatula to stir in the granulated sugar and vanilla until well mixed. Cover and refrigerate overnight.

To finish the cannoli, gently stir the chocolate chips into the ricotta filling. Fit a pastry bag with a large plain tip and fill with the ricotta mixture. Squeeze the filling into the two open sides of a cannolo shell so that it meets in the middle. (Alternatively, use a teaspoon to fill the shell from both ends, pushing some down into the middle.) Continue to fill the remaining shells.

Dust the filled cannoli generously with confectioners' sugar. If you wish to serve them as in Palermo, center a piece of candied orange peel on each cannolo. Serve immediately.

CONTINUED

HOW TO MAKE THE CRUNCHIEST, CREAMIEST CANNOLI

- Always keep the dough covered when you are not working with it to keep it moist and pliable, the secret to blistered, crispy shells.

- For the nicest-looking ends to show off the filling, look for the traditional Italian diamond-shape cannoli dough cutter. Or cut the dough with a round cookie cutter, then roll it with a pin to elongate the dough round into an oval approximately 4 inches by 5 inches.

- When using cannoli forms to make the shells, make sure the dough is loose rather than tightly rolled around the form. This creates a large enough opening to allow for plenty of filling, and it makes it easier to remove the form from the shell.

- The fried shells can be stored in an airtight container for up to 1 month.

- The quality of the ricotta is key to great cannoli; I recommend making your own, or purchasing sheep's milk ricotta if you can find it.

- Be sure the ricotta is very well drained. I drain mine overnight in the refrigerator, in a cheesecloth-lined strainer set over a bowl and covered.

- For a filling with the finest texture, use a firm but flexible plastic bowl scraper or the back of a spoon to press the ricotta through the finest strainer or screen you can find. I use a splatter screen. Whipping the ricotta or processing it in a food processor will not make it sufficiently smooth.

- Make the filling the day before you will fill and eat the cannoli.

- To prevent the chocolate from bleeding, wait to gently stir the chips into the ricotta until you are ready to fill the cannoli.

- To keep the shells crisp, fill the cannoli just before you serve them. In Palermo, the best shops fill them *espresso*, right in front of you, so that the filling remains creamy and the shell breaks crisply under your teeth. Once filled, the cannoli are best eaten within a couple of hours.

Sfince di San Giuseppe Saint Joseph's cream puffs

MAKES ABOUT 24 CREAM PUFFS

This dessert is typically served in Palermo on Saint Joseph's Day, March 19. They are similar to the Zeppole di San Giuseppe (page 107) made in Naples, but in Palermo the dough is fried in puffs and filled with ricotta cream.

To bake the *sfince* rather than frying them, pipe the dough into small dollops on a parchment paper–lined baking sheet and bake in a preheated 400°F (204°C) oven for about 25 minutes, until golden. Fill and serve as below.

Batter from Zeppole di San Giuseppe (page 107)

FILLING

4 cups (1.1 kg) ricotta cream (double recipe, page 188), refrigerated overnight

Vegetable oil, for frying

$^1/_2$ cup (85 g) semisweet or dark mini chocolate chips or finely chopped chocolate

Confectioners' sugar, for dusting (optional)

24 small pieces candied orange peel (page 193), for garnish (optional)

Prepare the batter, following the recipe used for Zeppole di San Giuseppe (page 107).

Heat 3 inches of oil to 350°F (177°C) in a deep pot or fryer. Fit a pastry bag with a $^7/_{16}$ inch plain tip, such as Ateco #805. Line a baking sheet with paper towels.

To form the *sfince,* lay out sheets of parchment paper on a flat surface and pipe the dough into 1$^1/_2$ inch mounds that are about 1 inch high, spacing them about 1 inch apart. Cut the parchment paper between the mounds to separate each dollop of batter onto its own piece of parchment paper.

To fry the *sfince,* carefully slip four mounds on their parchment paper into the hot oil, adjusting the heat to maintain a temperature of 350°F (177°C). Use tongs to pull the parchment paper from the oil as it separates from the *sfince*; let cool and discard. Use the tongs to continually turn the *sfince* as they puff up and brown, about 5 minutes. Many will split into two lobes, which is fine. Allow the oil to drip back into the pot before transferring the *sfince* to the prepared baking sheet as they are done. Continue to fry the remaining *sfince.*

Cool the *sfince* just until they can be easily handled, then use a small, sharp knife to cut them crosswise across the top to open them for filling. (If they have split into two lobes, cut across both.)

To make the filling, stir the chocolate chips into the refrigerated ricotta cream until they are evenly distributed.

To fill the *sfince,* fill a pastry bag fitted with a plain tip with the filling and use it to fill and slightly overflow the *sfince.* (Alternatively, you can fill the *sfince* with a spoon.) After filling, gently press the sides together and pipe a line of filling over the seam. Dust with confectioners' sugar, if you like. If you wish to serve them Palermo style, decorate the *sfince* by pressing a piece of candied orange peel into the exposed cream. Serve immediately, while still warm.

Gelo di Mandarino mandarin orange pudding

SERVES 4 | GLUTEN FREE

In Sicily you will find *gelo*—a chilled pudding thick enough to hold its shape—made using many of the area's favorite flavors: watermelon, coffee, cinnamon, orange, lemon, and mandarin orange. The puddings are typically thickened with wheat starch, but cornstarch works just as well. You can substitute other citrus juices, though if you choose something very tart, such as grapefruit or lime, omit the lemon juice and add sugar to your liking before adding the starch. For the most refreshing dessert, the *gelo* should be only mildly sweet.

You will need 2 to 3 pounds (900 g to 1.35 kg) of mandarin oranges in total. Before juicing the mandarins, set one aside for the garnish. To prepare the segments for the garnish, cut a slice from the top and bottom of the fruit, place one end flat against a cutting board, and follow the fruit's contour with your knife to remove all of the peel and pith. Holding the fruit over a bowl to catch the juices, use a paring knife to cut "supremes" from the mandarin orange by cutting along a segment to separate it from the membrane on both sides and releasing the flesh into the bowl. Continue to release all of the segments from the fruit and discard any seeds.

2 cups (480 ml) freshly squeezed mandarin orange juice

2 tablespoons freshly squeezed lemon juice

1/4 cup (50 g) sugar, or more to taste

1/4 cup (32 g) cornstarch or wheat starch

Segments cut from 1 mandarin orange, for garnish (see headnote)

Have ready four 4- to 6-ounce ramekins or molds.

Whisk together the mandarin juice, lemon juice, and sugar in a small, heavy saucepan over medium heat until the sugar dissolves completely. Taste and add more sugar, if you wish. Whisk in the cornstarch until it is completely dissolved.

Bring the mixture to a boil over medium heat, stirring constantly. Continue to cook and stir until the mixture is very thick, about 1 minute longer.

Before filling the ramekins, rinse them with water and shake out any excess. Divide the *gelo* evenly among the ramekins. Let it cool completely, then cover the ramekins with plastic wrap and refrigerate until they are set, at least 6 hours or up to 2 days.

Serve either in its ramekin or inverted onto a plate. To unmold, run a knife around the inside edge of the ramekin, then invert onto a dessert plate. Top with mandarin orange segments and serve cold.

Gelo di Mellone watermelon pudding

SERVES 8 | GLUTEN FREE

I have included two *gelo* recipes in this book because they are among the easiest desserts to make and are so refreshing. *Gelo di mellone* is typically served during il Festino di Santa Rosalia in mid-July, which celebrates the patron saint of Palermo, Sicily. Nowadays, in summer, you will find it in pastry shops throughout Palermo. The chocolate chips that top the pudding are meant to resemble the watermelon's black seeds. The pudding is often infused with the local jasmine that grows rampant throughout the city and decorated with a jasmine flower.

The *gelo* is simple and delicious on its own, but it is also lovely when used to fill the Crostata al Gelo di Mellone found on page 36.

About 6 cups (1.4 L) cubed flesh from 4 pounds (1.8 kg) seedless watermelon

1/2 cup (100 g) sugar, or more to taste

2/3 (85 g) cup cornstarch or wheat starch

Pinch of ground cinnamon

About 2 tablespoons semisweet or dark mini chocolate chips or chopped chocolate, for garnish

About 2 tablespoons chopped raw pistachios, for garnish

Have ready eight 6-ounce ramekins or molds.

Purée the watermelon in a blender until it is reduced to a liquid. Pour the purée through a strainer into a 4-cup measure, using a spoon to stir and press as much of the pulp through the strainer as possible. (Discard any remaining pulp; there should not be much.)

Pour 4 cups of the purée into a 2-quart heavy saucepan. (A bit more or less is no problem; if there is much more, enjoy it as refreshment.) Whisk in the sugar until it dissolves. Taste and add more sugar, if you wish. Whisk in the cornstarch and cinnamon until the starch is completely dissolved. Bring the mixture to a boil over medium heat, stirring constantly. Continue to cook and stir until the mixture is very thick, about 1 minute longer.

Before filling the ramekins, rinse them with water and shake out any excess. Divide the *gelo* evenly among the ramekins. Let it cool completely, then cover the ramekins with plastic wrap and refrigerate until they are set, at least 6 hours or up to 2 days.

Serve either in its ramekin or inverted onto a plate. To unmold, run a knife around the inside edge of the ramekin, then invert onto a dessert plate. Top with chopped chocolate and pistachios and serve cold.

Gelato al Cannolo cannoli ice cream

MAKES ABOUT 1 QUART (1 L)

When my niece, Ornella, recently visited from Italy, she found me in the kitchen making ricotta ice cream. "It tastes like mama's cannolo ice cream!" she exclaimed. I was intrigued, as I had never heard of a cannoli ice cream before, so I asked her to tell me more about it. She explained that it was very popular in the ice cream shops of Palermo, and that her mother had started making it at home by mixing broken cannoli shells and chocolate chips into a batch of her ricotta gelato. Ingenious!

For my version, I left the lemon zest and Strega liqueur out of my ricotta gelato recipe, then folded in my homemade cannoli shells (you can use store-bought, but homemade are best) and candied orange peel, along with a handful of mini chocolate chips. The result? It really does taste like eating a frozen cannolo. My niece, who generally won't touch candied orange peel, thought it was a brilliant addition. If you can find it, sheep's milk ricotta makes this Sicilian dessert even more authentic.

2 cups (454 g) fresh ricotta (page 186), well drained

$^3/_4$ cup (150 g) sugar

$^1/_2$ teaspoon pure vanilla extract

1 cup (240 ml) heavy cream

$^1/_4$ cup packed (50 g) finely chopped ($^1/_4$-inch) candied orange peel (page 193)

$^1/_4$ cup (40 g) semisweet or dark mini chocolate chips

3 (5-inch) cannoli shells, preferably homemade (page 53)

Combine the ricotta, sugar, and vanilla in a food processor and process until the mixture is very smooth. Scrape down the bowl with a spatula. With the processor running, add the cream through the feed tube until it is completely mixed in, about 30 seconds.

Transfer the mixture to an ice cream maker and freeze according to the manufacturer's directions. When frozen, transfer the gelato to a large bowl and use a spatula to stir in the orange peel and chocolate chips. Crumble the cannoli shells in large shards over the gelato; gently stir to distribute them evenly, allowing the shells to break down a bit without making crumbs of them.

Serve immediately, or transfer to an airtight container and freeze until ready to serve, preferably the day you make it, when the texture is at its creamiest. If the gelato freezes hard, let it soften in the refrigerator for 15 to 30 minutes before scooping.

Nero all'Arancia dark chocolate gelato with candied orange peel

MAKES ABOUT 1 QUART (1 L) | GLUTEN FREE

I fell in love with this ice cream while traveling in Sicily, where I sampled it in a number of towns. The version at Pasticceria Paradise in Palermo was so good that I inquired about the ingredients so I could create my own version. This gelato is made in the typical Sicilian style, by thickening milk (no cream) with cornstarch rather than egg yolks into what is called *crema rinforzata*. The cornstarch helps to prevent crystallization for a smooth, creamy ice cream that lets the flavor shine through. The combination of dark cocoa powder (I recommend Valrhona for the best flavor) and dark chocolate (Valrhona again) makes a rich, dark (*nero*) gelato. That, combined with the double punch of orange extract and candied orange peel, makes this my favorite chocolate ice cream.

3 cups (720 ml) whole milk

4 ounces (113 g) dark chocolate (about 70 percent cacao)

1/2 cup (54 g) unsweetened Dutch-processed cocoa powder

1 cup (200 g) sugar

3 tablespoons cornstarch

1/2 teaspoon pure orange extract

1/4 cup packed (50 g) finely chopped (1/4-inch) candied orange peel (page 193)

Bring 2 cups of the milk to a simmer in a medium saucepan. Remove from the heat and add the chocolate. Wait 2 minutes to allow the chocolate to melt and stir until smooth. Stir in the cocoa powder until well blended.

In a small bowl, whisk together the sugar, cornstarch, and the remaining 1 cup of milk until smooth. Stir the cornstarch mixture into the chocolate mixture.

Cook the mixture over medium heat, stirring constantly with a heatproof spatula, until it thickens to the texture of pudding, about 8 minutes. Transfer the mixture to a bowl set over a larger bowl filled with ice and water and let cool, stirring occasionally and taking care not to slosh water into the mixture, until cold.

Stir in the orange extract, then process the mixture in an ice cream machine according to the manufacturer's directions. When it is ready, use a spatula to fold in the chopped orange peel. Pack the ice cream into an airtight container and freeze until firm, at least 3 hours or up to 1 week, before serving.

Gelato Bianco Variegato al Pistacchio
white chocolate gelato with pistachio cream swirl

MAKES ABOUT 1¹/₂ QUARTS (1.5 L) | GLUTEN FREE

The town of Bronte at the foot of Mount Etna is prized for its flavorful, bright green pistachios, originally brought to Sicily by tenth-century Arab conquerors. The nuts are showcased in that town and throughout the island in all manner of desserts. This gelato recipe is from my sister-in-law, Giuseppina, who lives in Palermo and makes her own gelato at home. She adds flair and flavor to a white chocolate ice cream by swirling in a paste made from the sweetened pistachios.

The recipe calls for *crema di pistacchio,* a sweetened pistachio cream found in some upscale food stores, or ordered online (see Sources, page 203). For the best quality, make sure the paste comes from Bronte. *Pasta di pistacchio* is not right for this, but if you can't find the pistachio cream, try swirling chocolate-hazelnut paste (page 192) or other flavorings into the white chocolate gelato.

Choose a good-quality white chocolate, such as Valrhona or Guittard.

1 cup (240 ml) whole milk

4 large egg yolks

¹/₂ cup (100 g) sugar

6 ounces (170 g) white chocolate, coarsely chopped

1¹/₂ cups (240 ml) heavy cream

1 (6.3-ounce/180-g) jar crema di pistacchio (see headnote)

Bring the milk to a simmer in a heavy saucepan over medium heat. While it is heating, whisk the egg yolks and sugar in a bowl until thick and creamy. Slowly pour half of the hot milk into the egg mixture, whisking constantly as you pour.

Pour the milk and egg mixture back into the saucepan, again whisking constantly. Continue to cook and stir over medium heat until the mixture is thick enough to coat the back of a spoon. Remove from the heat, add the white chocolate, and let it stand for about 2 minutes to allow the chocolate to melt. Stir until completely smooth. Stir in the cream.

Transfer the mixture to a bowl set over a larger bowl filled with ice and water and let cool, stirring occasionally and taking care not to slosh water into the mixture, until cold.

Process the mixture in an ice cream machine according to the manufacturer's directions. When it is ready, transfer the ice cream to a bowl and gently stir in the *crema di pistacchio* to create swirls. Pack the ice cream into an airtight container and freeze until firm, at least 3 hours or up to 1 week, before serving.

2

Campania

The classic saying *Vedi Napoli e poi muori* (See Naples and then die), implying that you've experienced the best life has to offer, might as well refer to the city's unforgettable pastries. Naples is the capital city of Campania, and its sweets blend elements from the many cultures that have shaped its history: the Greeks, Romans, Normans, French, and Spanish. Like Palermo (Sicily), its place as capital of Italy and as an aristocratic seat in times past is reflected in the variety and opulence of the area's desserts.

Along with Sicily, Campania is one of the best known of the five Southern Italian regions. Its jaw-dropping Amalfi coastline is a popular tourist destination, with colorful buildings draped in bougainvillea perched on hillsides, and stairways winding down to the brilliant blue sea. Equally attractive are the mountainous Sorrento Peninsula and the island of Capri. As in Sicily, ancient historic and archeological sites showcase the area's rich history. Pizza may be its best-known food, but Naples has its iconic sweets as well.

Ask an Italian to name their favorite Neapolitan pastry and undoubtedly they will answer *sfogliatelle*—which might be crowned the "queen" dessert of Naples—or *babà*, the king. *Sfogliatelle* tops the hierarchy in its two forms: *Ricce* (page 101) and *Frolle* (page 98). Enclosed in different doughs, they hold the same filling of creamy ricotta mixed with cooked semolina, scented with cinnamon and studded with candied orange peel. This filling is said to have originated in the late 1600s or early 1700s, when a nun in the monastery of Santa Rosa Conca dei Marini, near Amalfi, was looking for a way to use up some leftover semo

lina cooked in milk. The story goes that she kneaded *strutto* (lard) into her bread dough, then used it to enclose the semolina filling, which she enriched with candied fruit and limoncello. She shaped the pastry in the form of a monk's hood and named her creation Santa Rosa after the convent. It wasn't until the early 1800s that the pastry traveled from Amalfi to Naples, where pastry chef Pintauro developed the sweet we know today and dubbed it *sfogliatelle* for the layers (*sfoglie*) of flaky pastry. Variations have developed over the years: If you purchase the pastry called

Santa Rosa today, the same hood-shaped case will be filled with pastry cream and seven *amarene* (preserved sour cherries). A version called *l'aragosta* (the lobster) is a *sfogliatella* with a long cream-filled tail. Still, the multilayered *Sfogliatelle Ricce* and the *Sfogliatelle Frolle* wrapped in pastry dough remain a Neapolitan icon throughout all of Italy.

The second pastry most associated with Naples is the *babà*, a soft yeasted cake soaked in rum. This one came with the *monsù* (a variation of the word *monsieur*), the chefs French royalty brought with them to the court in Naples. The traditional *babà* is baked as a large ring-shaped cake known as *ciambella* (similar to a Bundt or tube cake) or as individual cakes shaped like elongated mushrooms with round caps and long, tapered stems. Both are served filled or topped with whipped cream.

Here, as throughout Italy, desserts are often associated with a festival or saint's day. The 19th of March is the feast of San Giuseppe, honoring Saint Joseph, the father of Jesus, and celebrated throughout Italy as Father's Day. The story goes that Saint Joseph, the carpenter, fried dough (*frittelle*) as a second job, thus the dessert of choice on his saint's day is *Zeppole* (page 107)—fried or baked doughnuts. In modern times, the dough-nuts are filled with rich pastry cream and decorated with preserved amarena cherries.

Easter is celebrated with *Pastiera* (page 83), created to thank the mythical siren Parthenope, who inhabited the Gulf of Naples, for her spring-time songs. Made with wheat and ricotta, the dessert is a perfect expression of spring. Regional variations use rice or fresh pasta in place of the cooked wheat. As with many Italian desserts, *Pastiera* was once made only at home but now is often found in pastry shops, and not only at Easter but through-out the year, and in neighboring regions as well.

Ferragosto marks the beginning of the summer holiday season, when Italians frequently travel. The holiday coincides with Mary's assumption into heaven. The dessert of choice is *Melanzane al Cioccolato* (page 91), an unexpected combination of fried eggplant and chocolate that celebrates the beginning of the harvest season along the Amalfi Coast. In the Sorrento area, the holiday is celebrated with the stuffed pear dessert, *Pere Mast'Antuono Imbottite* (page 94), filled with sweetened ricotta.

As it is everywhere in Italy, the Christmas table is piled high with sweets, featuring assorted cookies and small fried *struffoli* dipped in honey, which came with the Greek occupation. Variations of these fried sweets are found throughout what was known as *Magna Grecia*, or Greater Greece, covering the entirety of Southern Italy. Many cookies are made only at this time, including the *rococo*, a hard cookie filled with the traditional Christmas spices of cinnamon, cloves, and orange, representing the wealth of flavors that arrived with the spice trade. The *mustacciolo* is a rhomboid-shaped cookie covered with chocolate icing, its name harkening back to a time when the dessert was sweetened with *mosto cotto* (page 197), or cooked grape must, before sugar was widely available.

Although Neapolitan desserts are some of Southern Italy's most popular, a great variety of pastries can be found throughout Campania, especially along the Amalfi Coast and the Sorrento Peninsula, where sweets are based on the large, thick-skinned local lemons, amarena cherries, walnuts, figs, and honey. Inland from Naples, in the provinces of Benevento and Avellino, grow some of the world's best hazelnuts, used in sweets such as the nut-studded *torrone* nougat. The city of Benevento is where Strega liqueur was born; the liqueur is colored with saffron and flavored with seventy different herbs, but the specific formula remains a secret even today. Many desserts here and throughout Italy are flavored with the much-loved liqueur.

La delizia al limone (lemon delight) is a modern creation from the 1970s, designed to showcase Sorrento's oversized, thick-skinned lemons, the same ones used to make the sweet liqueurs, limoncello and *rosolio di limone* (page 200). *Torta Caprese* (page 79) is the favorite chocolate and almond dessert named for the island of Capri; it is sometimes made with Amalfi lemons in place of the chocolate. Like Sicily, Campania is famous for its gelato, as well as for the semi-frozen *Coviglia* (page 109) popular in Naples in the late 1800s, its name taken from the bell-shaped aluminum container it was once served in. Nowadays, the dessert is served in a clear plastic cup that retains that classic shape.

La Deliziosa, page 74

Biscotti all'Amarena amarena cherry cookies

I've frequently seen these cookies in bakeries on my visits back to Calabria, but until I began researching Southern Italian sweets for this book, I'd never thought to consider how these Neapolitan cookies were made. As it turns out, their secret lies in transforming bakery leftovers into something new and enticing: the cookies are filled with a mixture of bakery scraps from Pan di Spagna, *cornetti,* and other cookies. The Italian baker can little afford to let these things go to waste, and happily, these cookies are very much in demand. You will find them not only in pastry shops but also in bread bakeries. To make large cookies as the Italians typically do, roll all of the pastry dough into a 9-inch by 14-inch rectangle, use all of the filling, and cut the log into 1-inch cookies, making about a dozen. I prefer the smaller ones I've formulated here.

Short-crust pastry (page 183, single crust)

1 layer (about 300 g) sponge cake, homemade (page 184) or store-bought

³/₄ cup (250 g) amarena cherry jam or sour cherry preserves, plus more for decorating

2 tablespoons unsweetened Dutch-processed cocoa powder

2 tablespoons white rum, Strega liqueur, or milk

Milk, as needed

GLAZE

1 large egg white

1 cup (125 g) confectioners' sugar, plus more if needed

Divide the pastry into two equal pieces, flatten each into a disk, and refrigerate for 1 hour. Roll one of the chilled dough pieces between two sheets of plastic wrap to make a 6-inch by 16-inch rectangle. Slide the wrapped, rolled dough onto a baking sheet and refrigerate while you roll out the second piece. Roll the second piece of dough in the same way; place on top of the first piece, wrapped, and refrigerate while you make the filling.

To make the filling, break up the sponge cake into the bowl of a food processor and process it into small crumbs. Add the jam, cocoa powder, and rum and process until evenly combined. Press a bit between your fingers—it should be moist and sticky, holding together when you gently squeeze it. If it is dry, add milk, 1 teaspoon at a time, mixing after each addition, until it holds together when pinched.

Take one rolled pastry sheet from the refrigerator, lay it on a flat surface, and peel off the top plastic. Use half of the filling to make a 2-inch-wide line lengthwise down the center of the dough. With a long side of the pastry facing you and using the plastic wrap as an aid, lift the side closest to you up and over the far side of the filling. Peel away the plastic from the bottom and repeat from the other side, overlapping the dough in the center to completely enclose the filling. Wrap and refrigerate the filled log until it is firm enough to cut, about 1 hour, or freeze for 20 minutes. Repeat to form a second log using the remaining pastry and filling.

Preheat the oven to 350°F (177°C) with racks in the upper and lower thirds of the oven. Line two baking sheets with parchment paper or silicone baking mats.

Unwrap one of the logs and place it seam side down on a flat surface. Cut the log crosswise at 1-inch intervals to make 16 slices. Evenly space the cookies, seam side down, on one of the baking sheets. Repeat with the second log and baking sheet.

Bake the cookies until they are firm and just starting to color, about 20 minutes, rotating the sheets front to back and top to bottom halfway through baking. While the cookies bake, make the glaze. Whisk the egg white vigorously in a bowl until it is quite frothy. Sift the confectioners' sugar over the top and continue whisking to make a thick glaze.

When the cookies are done, transfer the baking sheets to a flat, heat-proof surface, leaving the oven on. Brush the top of each cookie generously with the glaze (you won't need it all). To decorate the cookies as the Italians do, dip a toothpick into a small dish of cherry jam and run it crosswise over each cookie top to make two parallel lines about 1 inch apart. Return the baking sheets to the oven for another 5 minutes to set the glaze. Transfer the cookies on their sheets to wire racks to cool completely.

Pack the cookies into an airtight container, separating the layers with parchment paper, and store at room temperature for up to 2 weeks.

La Deliziosa sandwich cookies filled with hazelnut cream

MAKES ABOUT 28 2-INCH OR 14 3-INCH COOKIES

In Naples you will find these "delicious" treats made in both large and small sizes. I prefer the smaller ones because they are so rich. Making and filling the cookies a day ahead helps the cookies and filling to hold together properly when you take a bite.

The cookies are made with my favorite nut, the hazelnut, which my father used to bring home fresh from the field where he kept his goats. *Pasta di nocciola,* or hazelnut paste, is a nut butter made from toasted hazelnuts with a bit of oil added to allow it to blend. If you purchase hazelnut butter, make sure to find one with no added sugar or other ingredients—just hazelnuts and perhaps oil. You can also find *la deliziosa* filled with ricotta cream and chopped hazelnuts.

The filling and pastry can be made a day ahead and refrigerated separately overnight.

1 cup (226 g) unsalted butter

²/₃ cup (133 g) granulated sugar

1¹/₈ cups (320 g) pastry cream (page 185)

¹/₄ cup (60 g) hazelnut paste (pasta di nocciola), homemade (page 192) or store-bought

Short-crust pastry (page 183, double crust)

1 cup (150 g) skinned, toasted hazelnuts (page 189), chopped medium-fine

Confectioners' sugar, for finishing

Pictured on page 71

To make the filling, cream the butter and sugar in a small bowl using a handheld electric mixer until fluffy and well blended. Add the pastry cream at low speed. Mix in the hazelnut paste until well combined. Refrigerate the filling until very firm, at least 2 hours or up to a day.

Prepare the pastry dough, flatten the dough into a disk, wrap in plastic wrap, and chill for at least 1 hour.

Preheat the oven to 350°F (177°C) with racks in the upper and lower thirds of the oven. Line two baking sheets with parchment paper or silicone baking mats.

Roll the pastry to a thickness of ¹/₄ inch. Cut rounds with a 2- or 3-inch cookie cutter and transfer the rounds to the prepared baking sheets, spacing them 1 inch apart. (If the rounds are difficult to handle, refrigerate the dough until you can easily transfer them.) Reroll any remaining dough scraps to make additional cookies.

Bake the cookies until they are firm but have not begun to color, 10 to 12 minutes. (This keeps the cookies tender after they are formed.) Transfer the baking sheets to wire racks to cool completely.

To assemble the cookies, spread 1¹/₂ to 2 tablespoons of filling on the flat side of one cookie and top with the flat side of another cookie, gently pressing them together so that a bit of filling squeezes out the sides. Use a small offset spatula to smooth the filling over the edges, leaving a light coating over the cookie sides. Continue to fill all of the cookies.

Roll the sides of the cookies in the chopped hazelnuts to cover the entire edge and generously sift confectioners' sugar over the cookies.

Refrigerate the cookies until the filling is firm, preferably overnight. Serve cold.

Il Migliaccio Dolce di Carnevale semolina cake for Carnevale

SERVES 12

This dessert is traditionally prepared for Carnevale, the day before Lent begins, when Italians indulge in anticipation of the period of deprivation to follow. But don't wait for Fat Tuesday to enjoy *migliaccio,* a cross between two other Neapolitan classics: the filling from *Sfogliatelle* (page 101) and the flavors of *Pastiera* (page 83). You can find a simpler version without the ricotta, but this richer version is more in keeping with the spirit of the holiday.

Enjoyed warm, the *migliaccio* is a comforting pudding. If you have the patience, however, follow tradition and wait a day or two after making it before eating.

The name comes from the word *miglio,* dialect for corn, because this was once prepared with corn flour. For a taste of history, use fine cornmeal in place of the semolina, which also makes the dessert gluten free.

2 cups (454 g) fresh ricotta (page 186), well drained

3 cups (720 ml) whole milk

$^1/_2$ teaspoon kosher salt

1 cup (173 g) semolina

$^1/_4$ cup (57 g) unsalted butter

5 large eggs

1$^1/_2$ cups (300 g) granulated sugar

1 teaspoon pure vanilla extract

$^1/_2$ teaspoon ground cinnamon

Finely grated zest of 1 orange

Finely grated zest of 1 lemon

$^1/_2$ cup loosely packed (85 g) finely chopped ($^1/_4$-inch) candied orange peel (page 193)

Confectioners' sugar, for finishing

Press the ricotta through an ultrafine-mesh strainer or splatter screen (see page 14) into a bowl. Set aside.

Bring the milk and salt to a boil in a small saucepan over medium heat. Remove from the heat and add the semolina in a steady stream as you stir constantly with a whisk to discourage lumps from forming. Return the saucepan to medium heat and cook, stirring constantly, first with the whisk and then with a wooden spoon as the mixture thickens. Continue to cook and stir until the semolina begins to pull away from the sides of the pan and forms a thick paste, 2 to 3 minutes. Stir in the butter until it is completely incorporated. Transfer to a bowl to cool slightly.

Preheat the oven to 350°F (177°C) with a rack in the center of the oven. Butter a 10-inch springform pan.

Use a handheld electric mixer at medium speed to mix the eggs and granulated sugar in a bowl until well blended. Mix in the ricotta, vanilla, cinnamon, and orange and lemon zests until thoroughly incorporated. Add the cooled semolina, beating until all the clumps have been broken up and the mixture is smooth. Stir in the candied orange peel.

Turn the mixture into the prepared pan and smooth the top. Bake until puffed, golden, and slightly jiggly only near the center, about 90 minutes. Transfer the pan to a rack to cool. When partially cooled (but still somewhat warm), remove the outer ring of the pan and sift confectioners' sugar over the surface. (The cake will fall somewhat as it cools.) Enjoy warm or at room temperature, or wait until it has cooled completely, refrigerate, and enjoy cold.

Torta Ricotta e Pere ricotta and pear cake

SERVES 12 | GLUTEN FREE

I don't recall seeing a cake made by sandwiching a chilled filling of ricotta and pears between layers of dacquoise while growing up in Calabria, so when I sampled this cake at the restaurant La Locanda del Re while visiting the town of Santa Severina, I assumed it was a modern invention of the chef's. On a trip back to Calabria several years later, I learned that the dessert originated in the late 1990s with renowned pastry chef Sal De Riso in the town of Minori. Because I had so enjoyed the cake in Santa Severina, I was curious to try De Riso's original, so off I went to hunt it down at his pastry shop. Along the way, I found variations of the cake throughout Southern Italy, even coming across a gelato made with ricotta and pears. What struck me in the first version I'd tried were the crunchy layers encasing the filling, rather than the soft layers of *pan di Spagna* (sponge cake) I tasted at De Riso's pastry shop. This cake has become popular all over Southern Italy, where you will find the layers made with plain *pasta frolla,* hazelnut *pasta frolla,* or hazelnut dacquoise, as I have used here.

HAZELNUT DACQUOISE

1 cup plus 2 tablespoons (160 g) raw, skin-on hazelnuts

³/₄ cup plus 1 tablespoon (100 g) confectioners' sugar, plus more for finishing

4 large egg whites

Pinch of kosher salt

¹/₂ cup plus 2 tablespoons (125 g) granulated sugar

PEAR FILLING

1 pound (454 g) ripe Bartlett pears, peeled, cored, and cut into ¹/₂-inch pieces

¹/₃ cup (67 g) granulated sugar

2 tablespoons fresh lemon juice

1 tablespoon pear liqueur

RICOTTA MOUSSE

2 cups (454 g) fresh ricotta (page 186), well drained

³/₄ cup (150 g) granulated sugar

1 teaspoon pure vanilla extract

1 cup plus 2 tablespoons (270 ml) heavy cream

2 sheets silver grade gelatin

To make the dacquoise layers, preheat the oven to 350°F (177°C) with racks in the upper and lower thirds of the oven. Line two baking sheets with parchment paper. Using a 9-inch cake pan as a guide, draw a circle in pencil on each piece of parchment paper, then turn over the parchment paper so that the writing can be seen through the paper. Lightly oil the parchment paper inside and slightly beyond the two circles with safflower oil or another neutral-tasting oil.

Combine the hazelnuts and confectioners' sugar in a food processor and process until the nuts are the texture of medium-fine cornmeal, scraping down the bowl as needed.

Beat the egg whites with the salt at medium speed in a stand mixer fitted with the whisk attachment until they form soft peaks. With the mixer running, add the granulated sugar in a few additions, then increase the speed to high and beat until peaks form that are firm but not at all dry. (Alternatively, use a handheld electric mixer.) Use a large spatula to fold in the hazelnuts in three additions, until they are fully incorporated.

Divide the dacquoise mixture equally between the two baking sheets, spreading it with a small offset spatula to fill the circles in an even layer all the way to the edges. Bake until the layers are dry to the touch and light golden all over, 25 to 30 minutes, rotating the pans top to bottom and front to back halfway through baking.

CONTINUED

Transfer the layers on their parchment paper liners to a flat surface. The cakes will have expanded slightly: to ensure they will fit into the pan, trim all around the edges of the warm layers with a sharp paring knife, using a 9-inch cake pan as a guide. Slide the layers onto a wire rack to cool completely.

To prepare the filling, put the pears in a small nonstick skillet and add the sugar and lemon juice. Stir over high heat until the fruit is translucent, 8 to 10 minutes. Remove from the heat and stir in the liqueur. Transfer the fruit to a small strainer placed over a bowl and set aside to cool.

To make the ricotta mousse, press the ricotta through an ultrafine-mesh strainer or splatter screen (see page 14) into a large bowl. Use a spatula to stir in the granulated sugar and vanilla until well mixed.

In a separate bowl, whip 1 cup of the cream using an electric mixer until firm peaks form. Use a large spatula to fold the whipped cream into the ricotta mixture; set aside.

Put the gelatin into a small bowl of cool water to completely submerge it; let stand for 5 minutes to soften. Heat the remaining 2 tablespoons of cream in a bowl in the microwave or in a small saucepan over medium heat until it simmers. Squeeze the water from the soaked gelatin and stir it into the hot cream until it dissolves completely. Stir 1/4 cup of the ricotta mixture into the dissolved gelatin, then use a large spatula to fold this mixture back into the ricotta until well mixed. Gently fold the cooled drained pears into the ricotta mousse. (Discard the pear syrup or reserve for another use.) Cover the mousse and refrigerate for 2 hours.

To assemble the cake, place a dacquoise round top side up in a 9-inch springform pan. Spread the ricotta-pear filling over the cake, leveling the top. Top with the second cake. Cover the pan tightly with plastic wrap and refrigerate until set, at least 4 hours or up to a day. (The assembled cake may be frozen in the pan for up to 1 month. Transfer to the refrigerator to thaw overnight, then let stand at room temperature for 1 hour before serving.)

To serve, release the outer ring from the pan and transfer the cake on its base to a serving platter, or use a large spatula to transfer the cake directly to the platter. Dust the cake generously with confectioners' sugar and cut into wedges with a sharp serrated knife.

Torta Caprese flourless chocolate almond cake

SERVES 12 | GLUTEN FREE

This rich cake takes its name from the island of Capri, where it originated. Many tales are told of the way the cake came about, perhaps the most charming of which recounts a visit to Capri in the 1920s from a group of Mafia men on behalf of Al Capone. Pastry chef Carmine Di Fiore was mortified when he realized he'd forgotten the flour in the cake, but the mobsters liked the moist, chocolaty confection so much they asked for its name. Di Fiore quickly replied, "Torta Caprese!" and it has kept that name ever since. The cake is renowned on the island and throughout the Amalfi Coast.

Pastry shops and home bakers often add a hint of liqueur, which is entirely optional; I like it with Kahlúa, but Strega is more common on the Amalfi Coast.

8 ounces (226 g) dark chocolate (55 to 60 percent cacao)

1²/₃ cups (250 g) skin-on almonds

1 cup (226 g) unsalted butter, softened

1 cup (200 g) granulated sugar

5 large eggs, separated

2 tablespoons coffee liqueur, such as Kahlúa (optional)

Pinch of kosher salt

Confectioners' sugar or whipped cream, for serving

Preheat the oven to 325°F (163°C) with a rack in the center. Butter a 10-inch springform pan.

Melt the chocolate in a double boiler or in a bowl placed over, but not touching, about an inch of simmering water. Set aside until cool. Process the almonds in a food processor until they have the texture of coarse cornmeal, stopping before they are as fine as flour.

Mix the butter with about half of the sugar in the bowl of a stand mixer fitted with the whisk attachment at medium speed until smooth, scraping the bowl as needed. Add the yolks, one at a time, beating and scraping the bowl between additions. At low speed, mix in the liqueur, if using, and the melted chocolate until well blended, then mix in the ground almonds. (Alternatively, use a handheld electric mixer.)

Beat the egg whites and salt in a clean bowl using a clean whisk attachment at medium speed until they form soft peaks. Gradually add the remaining ¹/₂ cup sugar, a little at a time, then continue to beat at high speed until firm peaks form that are not at all dry.

Using a large spatula, fold one-third of the egg whites into the chocolate mixture to lighten it, then gently fold in the remaining whites until no streaks remain. Spread the batter evenly in the prepared pan.

Bake until a toothpick inserted in the center comes out with just a few moist crumbs clinging to it, 50 to 55 minutes. Set the pan on a wire rack to cool. Once cool, run a knife around the edge of the cake, then release and remove the ring. Transfer the cake on the pan bottom to a serving plate, as I prefer, or invert onto the serving plate as they do in Capri.

To serve, dust the top of the cake with confectioners' sugar, or top with a dollop of whipped cream.

Scazzetta del Cardinale sponge cake filled with pastry cream and strawberries

SERVES 12

This classic dessert found in the pastry shops of Salerno is cloaked in strawberry glaze to resemble the cardinal's pink skullcap, or *zucchetto*. In local dialect, the cap is called a *scazzetta* for the way in which it is pressed against the back of the head. (The cake is also known as *scazzetta del vescovo,* or bishop's cap.) The cake is commonly decorated with a few tiny strawberries to resemble the little knot atop the *scazzetta*.

This cake originated at Pasticceria Pantaleone in Salerno, where the sponge cake is filled with crema Chantilly (pastry cream mixed with whipped cream) and wild alpine strawberries and covered in a pink confectioners' sugar glaze.

SOAKING SYRUP

^{1}/₃ cup (66 g) granulated sugar

^{1}/₃ cup (80 ml) water

^{1}/₄ cup (60 ml) Strega liqueur

CAKE

1 pint (227 g) strawberries, preferably the wild alpine variety, stemmed

1 tablespoon granulated sugar (optional)

1 tablespoon fresh lemon juice (optional)

1 (9-inch) sponge cake (page 184), cooled

CREMA CHANTILLY

^{1}/₂ cup (120 ml) heavy cream

1 tablespoon granulated sugar

1^1/₈ cups (320 g) pastry cream (page 185), cooled

GLAZE

^{1}/₂ pint (113 g) strawberries, stemmed

1 tablespoon fresh lemon juice

1^1/₂ cups (188 g) confectioners' sugar

4 to 6 tiny stem-on alpine strawberries, for garnish, plus additional strawberries, if desired

To prepare the soaking syrup, stir the granulated sugar with the water in a small saucepan. Bring the mixture to a boil and stir to dissolve the sugar. Stir in the Strega and set aside to cool.

To make the cake, if you are using common strawberries, cut them into ^{1}/₂-inch dice and combine them with the sugar and lemon juice in a small bowl. Mix and let stand for 15 minutes. (If using alpine or other super-sweet, flavorful berries, omit the sugar and lemon. Alpine berries also needn't be cut.)

To make the crema Chantilly, whip the cream with the granulated sugar using an electric mixer until firm peaks form. Use a large spatula to fold in the pastry cream. Set aside.

Line a 9- by 2-inch round cake pan (the one you baked the sponge cake in is best) with plastic wrap, leaving the ends hanging over the sides of the pan. Using a long serrated knife with a sawing motion, turning the cake as you cut, cut the cake horizontally into two even layers. Place the top layer cut side up in the prepared pan and brush or spoon half of the soaking syrup evenly over the cake. Spread all of the crema Chantilly evenly over the cake, all the way to the edges. Drain the berries if you soaked them, and arrange the berries evenly over the crema. Invert the bottom cake layer, cut side down, over the berries and brush the top with the remaining soaking syrup. Fold over the overhanging plastic wrap to cover the cake, pressing it directly against the surface. Refrigerate for 8 hours, or overnight.

After the cake has chilled, make the glaze. Combine the ^{1}/₂ pint of strawberries with the lemon juice in a blender and process to make a smooth purée. Put the confectioners' sugar into a bowl and stir in 2 tablespoons of strawberry purée. Continue to add the strawberry purée, a tablespoon at a time, to make a smooth, thick glaze. (Discard any remaining purée or save for another use.)

Set a wire rack over a rimmed baking sheet to catch the dripping glaze. Peel away and fold back the plastic from the top of the cake. Invert the cake onto a 9-inch cardboard cake round, the base of a 9-inch tart pan, or a flat 9-inch plate. (The base should not extend beyond the cake.) Remove the plastic wrap and set the cake on its base on the wire rack.

Pour the glaze over the cake, starting at the center and gradually moving in a spiral pattern toward the edges to completely cover the top and sides of the cake. Pour additional glaze over any uncovered spots on the side of the cake to cover them completely, retrieving some of the glaze with a spatula from the pan below, if needed. Transfer the cake on its base to a serving plate and refrigerate until the glaze sets, at least 2 hours or up to 1 day.

Before serving, place the stem-on strawberries in the center of the cake. For the prettiest finish, decorate the sides of the cake with sliced strawberries, pointed ends up.

La Pastiera Napoletana Easter pie with wheat berries and ricotta

SERVES 12 TO 16

Pastiera is typically served for Easter, but some say it originated from a pagan tradition that pre-dates the Christian Easter holiday. Others say it reflects ancient Roman celebrations of spring-time and rebirth. Still another legend suggests that the dish was created to thank the siren Parthenope, who lived in the Gulf of Naples, for her springtime songs.

Whatever its origin, it is clear that the dessert is meant to celebrate spring—made with wheat, which begins to sprout at this time, ricotta made with fresh sheep's milk, fragrant orange flower water, and eggs symbolizing fertility and rebirth. Tradition instructs us to prepare the *pastiera* three days in advance of Easter, symbolizing the time between Christ's death and resurrection. But there is a better reason for the waiting period: it allows the flavors and textures to marry.

Traditionally, the *pastiere* were baked in community ovens on the Thursday before Easter. Families would never prepare just one, but rather would bake many to share with family and friends. Nowadays, you can find *pastiera* in the pastry shops of Naples all year long.

In Italy, this is made with the jarred cooked wheat called *grano cotto,* available through Amazon.com or in Italian food shops. To use raw hulled wheat berries instead, cover $^1/_2$ cup (100 g) wheat berries with 2 cups cold water in a bowl. Cover and let stand at room tempera-ture for 3 days, draining off and replacing the water daily. Drain the wheat berries, transfer them to a saucepan, and add 3 cups of water and $^1/_2$ teaspoon of kosher salt. Gently boil until the wheat berries are tender and most have split, about 90 minutes, adding water if needed to keep them covered. Let cool completely in the water, then drain.

Short-crust pastry (page 183, double crust)

1$^3/_4$ cups (454 g) fresh ricotta (page 186), well drained

1$^1/_3$ cups (325 g) grano cotto (see headnote), drained

1$^3/_4$ cups (420 ml) whole milk, plus more if needed

1$^1/_2$ cups (312 g) plus 1 table-spoon granulated sugar

1 tablespoon unsalted butter

Finely grated zest of 2 lemons

$^1/_2$ vanilla bean, split

3 large eggs, separated

2 large egg yolks

1 tablespoon orange flower water

Finely grated zest of 1 orange

$^1/_2$ cup packed (100 g) finely chopped ($^1/_4$-inch) candied orange peel (page 193)

Confectioners' sugar, for finishing

Prepare the pastry dough. Divide the dough into two pieces, one slightly larger than the other, flatten into disks, wrap in plastic wrap, and chill for at least 1 hour.

Press the ricotta through an ultrafine-mesh strainer or splatter screen (see page 14) into a bowl. Set aside.

Butter a 10-inch springform pan or deep-dish pie pan.

Put the cooked, drained wheat (*grano cotto)* into a heavy 2-quart saucepan. Stir in the milk, 1 tablespoon of the sugar, the butter, and the zest of 1 lemon. Scrape in the vanilla seeds and drop in the pod. Bring the mixture to a boil over medium heat, then reduce the heat and simmer, stirring occasionally, until the grains are very soft and the liquid forms a thick, creamy sauce, about 50 minutes for the jarred grains or up to an hour for the cooked whole grains. Stir more fre-quently toward the end to prevent scorching, and add a bit more milk if the mixture becomes dry. Transfer the wheat mixture to a shallow bowl and let cool. Remove and discard the vanilla pod.

CONTINUED

While the wheat cooks, roll the pastry dough. Leaving the smaller disk in the refrigerator, roll the larger disk between two sheets of plastic wrap into a 13-inch round. Remove the plastic from one side and invert the dough over the prepared pan, nestling it evenly into the bottom and sides. Refrigerate the covered pastry in the pan. Roll the second disk into a 10^1/$_2$-inch round on a sheet of parchment paper. Use a fluted cutter to cut the dough into ^{3}/$_4$-inch-wide strips, making at least 10 strips. Slide the dough on the parchment paper onto a rimless baking sheet and refrigerate.

Preheat the oven to 325°F (163°C) with a rack in the center of the oven.

To make the filling, in a clean bowl using clean beaters, beat the 3 egg whites with an electric mixer at high speed until firm peaks form that are not at all dry.

In a large bowl, mix the ricotta with the remaining 1^1/$_2$ cups granulated sugar at medium-low speed until smooth. Mix in the 5 yolks, the orange flower water, the orange zest, and the zest of the remaining lemon. Use a large spatula to stir in the cooled wheat and the candied peel. Fold in the beaten egg whites in three additions.

PASTIERA VARIATIONS

Many types of *pastiera* are found throughout Campania. This traditional style originated in Naples. The popular Sorrento style is made by folding a cup of pastry cream (page 185) into the filling. Pastiera di Spaghetti (page 88) is made with cooked pasta standing in for the wheat berries (page 83). I also came across a version from Benevento made with rice.

As with most Italian recipes, each family seems to have its own way of making this well-liked dessert—some pass all or a portion of the filling through a food mill for a soft, uniform texture. Others add a pinch of cinnamon. Some use whole eggs rather than beating the whites separately. Still others use candied citron in place of the orange peel, or leave out the candied fruit altogether. I make all of my lattice tops using five pastry strips in each direction. If you prefer, you can make the more traditional *pastiera* presentation shown in the photo using three strips in each direction. Note that Italians do not weave the lattice, but rather place the first set of strips in one direction, then lay the second set on top.

Spread the filling evenly in the dough-lined pan. Place the strips of pastry over the top, spacing five strips evenly in one direction, then place the remaining five strips at about a 45-degree angle over the top, without weaving, to form a diamond pattern. Using the fluted cutter, trim the dough around the edges to about $1/2$ inch above the filling. Fold the excess bottom dough over the strips, pressing the strips and bottom dough together to seal them.

Bake until the top is deep golden brown and the center no longer jiggles when you shake the pan, 90 to 100 minutes. If the edges brown too quickly, shield them with strips of aluminum foil.

When it is ready, turn off the oven, prop the oven door open, and leave the *pastiera* inside until it has cooled completely.

When cool, run a knife around the edge, then release and remove the pan sides. Transfer the *pastiera* on its base to a plate. (If you used a pie pan, leave the *pastiera* in the pan.) Cover tightly and refrigerate for three days before serving. Let the *pastiera* stand at room temperature for 45 to 60 minutes before serving.

To serve, dust the top lightly with confectioners' sugar and cut into wedges.

Pastiera di Spaghetti Easter pie made with spaghetti

I owe this recipe to Patrick O'Boyle, a man from New Jersey whose grandmother's parents immigrated to the United States from Piano di Sorrento and Arzano in 1901. Pat's mother, like his grandmother before her, still makes dozens of *pastiere* to share with family and friends every Easter, a great tradition that sadly has been lost, not only here but also in Italy. I hadn't heard of his version of the traditional Easter dessert and was intrigued that it used cooked spaghetti. The pastry cream is used in Sorrento, and the spaghetti is typical of towns outside of Naples, at the foot of Mount Vesuvius. In these towns, often only the elderly still make *pastiera* using pasta; the younger generation has adopted the Neapolitan tradition of using wheat berries, if they make it at all. This recipe was Pat's grandmother's amalgamation of her parents' traditions. I love *amarene*, the Italian sour cherries preserved in syrup, so was pleased to see them in this pie; substitute candied orange peel if you prefer.

Short-crust pastry (page 183, single crust)

3 cups (680 g) fresh ricotta (page 186), well drained

8 ounces (227 g) spaghetti

4 large eggs, separated

2 large egg yolks

1 1/2 cups (300 g) granulated sugar

1 teaspoon pure vanilla extract

Finely grated zest of 1 lemon

Finely grated zest of 1 orange

1 tablespoon orange flower water

1 1/8 cups (315 g) pastry cream (page 185)

1/2 cup preserved amarena cherries, drained and cut in half

Confectioners' sugar, for finishing

Make the pastry dough, flatten into a disk, wrap in plastic wrap, and chill for at least 1 hour.

Press the ricotta through an ultrafine-mesh strainer or splatter screen (see page 14).

Preheat the oven to 325°F (163°C) with a rack in the center of the oven. Butter a 10-inch springform pan or a 12-inch deep-dish pie pan.

Cook the spaghetti in plenty of salted water according to the package directions. It should be completely cooked but not mushy. Drain, rinse with cold water, drain again, and set aside.

Cover the pastry dough with plastic wrap and roll out on a sheet of parchment paper into a 10-inch round. Use a fluted cutter to cut the dough into 3/4-inch-wide strips, making at least 10 strips. Slide the covered dough on the parchment paper onto a rimless baking sheet and refrigerate.

In a clean bowl using clean beaters, beat the egg whites at high speed with an electric mixer until firm peaks form that are not at all dry.

In a large bowl, mix the ricotta and granulated sugar at medium-low speed until smooth. Add the 6 egg yolks, vanilla, lemon and orange zest, and orange flower water. Mix in the pastry cream until smooth. Stir in the spaghetti and cherries with a large spatula, mixing until the spaghetti is well coated. Fold in the beaten egg whites in three additions.

Spread the filling evenly in the pan, distributing the cherries as evenly as possible. Place the strips of pastry over the top, spacing five strips evenly in one direction, then placing the remaining five strips at about a 45-degree angle over the top, without weaving, to form a diamond pattern. Using the fluted cutter, trim the dough around the edges to about $1/2$ inch above the filling. Fold the excess bottom dough over the strips, pressing the top strips and bottom dough together to seal them.

Bake until the top is deep golden brown and the center no longer jiggles when you shake the pan, about 90 minutes. If the edges brown too quickly, shield them with strips of aluminum foil.

When it is ready, turn off the oven, prop the oven door open, and leave the *pastiera* inside until it has cooled completely.

When cool, run a knife around the edge, then release and remove the pan sides. Transfer the *pastiera* on its base to a plate. (If you used a pie pan, leave the *pastiera* in the pan.) Cover tightly and refrigerate for 3 days before serving.

To serve, let the *pastiera* stand at room temperature for 45 to 60 minutes. Dust lightly with confectioners' sugar and cut into wedges.

Melanzane al Cioccolato eggplant layered with sweetened ricotta and chocolate sauce

Eggplant? For dessert? Indeed, this specialty of the Amalfi Coast found only in the summer months is traditionally served on August 15th to celebrate the summer holiday, Ferragosto, which falls at the height of the eggplant harvest. In the most common version, the eggplant is filled simply with sweetened almonds, amaretti, orange, and chocolate and is often accompanied by a small glass of iced limoncello. I was delighted to find this variation in Maiori, along the Amalfi Coast, where the eggplant is layered with a ricotta custard filling and chocolate sauce, then baked and chilled before being topped with more chocolate sauce.

This makes a charming dessert for a dinner party when made in individual servings: Layer the eggplant and filling in small ramekins, spreading the ricotta filling in a $1/4$-inch-thick layer. To serve, invert the desserts from the ramekins onto dessert plates.

3 pounds (1.36 kg) globe eggplant, peeled (3 eggplants)

About $1/2$ cup all-purpose flour, for coating

$1^1/4$ cups (250 g) sugar, plus more for the baking dish

$1/2$ teaspoon ground cinnamon

Finely grated zest of 2 lemons

Extra-virgin olive oil, for frying

RICOTTA FILLING

1 cup (248 g) fresh ricotta (page 186), well drained

$1/4$ cup (50 g) sugar

$1/3$ cup (50 g) blanched almonds (page 189), toasted and finely chopped

$1/3$ cup (28 g) crushed amaretti, from about 9 small amaretti cookies

2 tablespoons packed finely chopped ($1/4$-inch) candied orange peel (page 193)

2 large eggs, lightly beaten

CHOCOLATE SAUCE

1 cup (240 ml) heavy cream

8 ounces (227 g) good-quality dark chocolate (55 to 65 percent cacao), coarsely chopped

Generously butter a 9- by 2-inch square baking dish and coat with sugar, knocking out the excess.

Stand an eggplant on a cutting board and cut a $1/4$-inch slice, top to bottom. Lay the eggplant on the cut side and cut lengthwise into $1/4$-inch-thick slices. Cut the remaining eggplant(s) in the same manner.

Put the flour in a large, shallow pan. Mix the sugar, cinnamon, and lemon zest in another large, shallow pan.

Heat $1/2$ inch of olive oil in a 10-inch skillet to 350°F (177°C). The oil should sizzle when you drop in a small piece of eggplant. Line a baking sheet with paper towels and place it near the stove.

Lightly coat an eggplant slice with flour, knocking off the excess, and fry, turning until the eggplant is light golden on both sides. Allow the oil to drip back into the pot before transferring the eggplant to the prepared baking sheet. Continue to fry all of the eggplant, fitting as many slices in the pan as you can without crowding, and placing paper towels between layers of the fried eggplant as needed.

While the eggplant is still warm, press each slice into the cinnamon-sugar mixture to coat both sides. Transfer the slices to a baking sheet and set aside until you are ready to assemble the dessert.

To make the filling, press the ricotta through an ultrafine-mesh strainer or splatter screen (see page 14) into a bowl. Stir in the sugar, almonds, amaretti, and orange peel. Mix in the eggs and set aside.

To make the chocolate sauce, heat the cream in a small saucepan over medium heat until it steams and bubbles around the edges.

CONTINUED

Remove from the heat and add the chocolate. Let stand 2 minutes to melt, then stir until smooth.

Preheat the oven to 375°F (190°C) with a rack in the center of the oven.

To assemble the dish, arrange the fried and coated eggplant slices around the perimeter of the dish so that they cover the sides, with about half of each slice draping over the edge of the dish all around. Cover the bottom of the pan with a few small slices. Spread one-third of the ricotta filling over the eggplant in the bottom of the dish, drizzle with one-quarter of the chocolate sauce, and top with a layer of eggplant. Repeat the layers of ricotta, chocolate, and eggplant two more times, ending with the eggplant. Fold the draped eggplant slices up and over the top to enclose the filling. Reserve the remaining sauce for serving.

Place the dish on a baking sheet to catch any liquid that bubbles over and bake until hot and bubbling, about 20 minutes. Let cool completely, then cover and refrigerate until it is completely cold, at least 4 hours, or overnight.

To serve, let the dish stand at room temperature for about an hour to take the chill off. Cut the filled eggplant into four strips in one direction and three in the other to make twelve pieces. Use a flexible spatula or server to transfer the pieces to individual dessert plates. Warm the remaining chocolate sauce just until it is pourable and drizzle over each serving.

Refrigerate leftovers, covered, for up to 3 days.

Pizza di Amarene tart filled with pastry cream and amarena cherries

SERVES 8 TO 10

This rich crostata filled with pastry cream and tart cherries looks like a deep-dish pizza, thus its name. The pizza is a specialty of Naples but is found all over Campania. When sold as tartlets, it is known as *pasticciotto con crema e amarene*.

Look for the jarred Italian sour cherries in syrup known as *amarene* at specialty food shops (see Sources, page 203). You will need about 36 of them, but the count need not be exact.

This is a great recipe for making ahead because it is even better the day after it is baked.

Short-crust pastry (page 183, double crust)

2¹/₄ cups (640 g) pastry cream (page 185)

1 (8.8-ounce/130 g) jar amarena cherries in syrup, drained

1 large egg

1 tablespoon granulated sugar

Confectioners' sugar, for dusting

Prepare the pastry and divide the dough into two pieces, one slightly larger than the other. Flatten the pieces into disks, wrap in plastic wrap, and chill for at least 1 hour.

Preheat the oven to 375°F (190°C) with a rack in the center of the oven. Butter the bottom and sides of a 9-inch fluted tart pan with a removable bottom and at least 1-inch sides. Dust with flour, knocking out the excess.

Roll out the larger pastry disk between two sheets of plastic wrap to make an 12-inch round. Peel off the top sheet of plastic and invert the dough, centering it over the prepared pan. Using the sheet of plastic wrap that is now on top as an aid, settle the dough into the pan so that it covers the bottom and comes all the way up the sides. Remove the plastic wrap and trim the pastry flush with the edge; set the tart pan aside.

Roll the second pastry disk between two sheets of plastic wrap to make a 9-inch round. Set aside.

Spread half of the pastry cream evenly over the dough in the pan. Distribute the cherries evenly over the pastry cream, then spread the remaining pastry cream to (mostly) cover them. Peel the top sheet of plastic wrap from the second dough round and invert the dough over the pan. Remove the plastic wrap and fold the sides of the dough over the top, pressing to seal the top and bottom crusts all around.

In a small bowl, whisk the egg and granulated sugar, then brush the egg wash over the top of the tart. Bake until the pastry is deep golden all over, about 35 minutes. Transfer the tart pan to a wire rack to cool. When it is cool enough to handle, drop away the pan sides, leaving the tart on the base. Let cool completely, for several hours or overnight.

To serve, dust the top of the "pizza" with confectioners' sugar and cut into wedges.

Pere Mast'Antuono Imbottite ricotta-filled baked pears

SERVES 6

When I asked Sorrento-based writer Angie Cafiero for a traditional dessert from her area for this book, she suggested this unusual family recipe, prepared on August 15, the day of the Assumption of the Virgin Mary and the beginning of Ferragosto, the national vacation time in Italy.

The dessert takes its name from the local pear variety, Mast'Antuono, which reaches its peak harvest in mid-August. The story goes that a farmer had a pear tree that would never produce fruit. In frustration, the man cut down the tree and sold the wood to a sculptor, who carved the trunk into a statue of St. Anthony and had it installed in his church. When the farmer learned of the statue, he went to the church and implored of the wood statue, "You are the very tree that would produce no pears. Now that you pose as St. Anthony, how am I to believe that you can perform great acts of grace?" The story lives on as an Italian proverb that describes someone who appears to be a good and holy person, but actually is not.

Pere Mast'Antuono are small and round, almost like an apple. Choose a similarly round and squat pear variety that allows room for the filling, such as the Comice. The stuffed pears are often served smothered in chocolate sauce, but I prefer them on their own, or lightly drizzled with chocolate.

6 firm-ripe pears

$^1/_2$ cup (114 g) fresh ricotta (page 186), well drained

1 large egg

$^1/_2$ cup (50 g) crushed amaretti, from about 17 small amaretti cookies

5 tablespoons (86 g) almond paste, homemade (page 190) or store-bought

2 tablespoons packed finely chopped ($^1/_4$-inch) candied orange peel (page 193)

$^1/_4$ teaspoon ground cinnamon

$^1/_4$ teaspoon pure vanilla extract

$^1/_2$ cup (120 ml) sweet vermouth or sweet white wine

2 tablespoons sugar

$^1/_2$ cup (120 ml) water

Chocolate Sauce (page 91), optional

Preheat the oven to 400°F (204°C) with a rack in the center of the oven. Have an 8-inch square baking pan ready.

Cut off the top inch of each pear and set aside for later. Use a melon baller or spoon to scoop out the flesh, leaving about $^1/_4$ inch all around and taking care not to poke through the bottoms. Discard the seeds and tough cores and finely chop the flesh; set aside.

Press the ricotta through an ultrafine-mesh strainer or a splatter screen (see page 14) into a bowl. Stir in the egg. Stir in the amaretti, almond paste, orange peel, cinnamon, and vanilla. Add the chopped pears and stir to combine everything evenly.

Place the pears in the prepared baking pan and fill the cavities with the ricotta filling. Replace the tops on the pears.

Stir together the vermouth, sugar, and water in a measuring cup or bowl, then pour the mixture into the pan to surround the pears. Bake until the pears are soft and beginning to collapse, about 75 minutes. The filling will puff out and lightly brown between pears and their tops. Remove from the oven and spoon some of the sauce over the pears for a pretty sheen. Let cool in the pan to room temperature, then refrigerate until cold, several hours or overnight.

Serve the chilled pears in shallow bowls, drizzled with chocolate sauce, if you wish.

Mousse di Ricotta al Mosto Cotto
ricotta mousse with grape must syrup

SERVES 6 | GLUTEN FREE

A light-textured mousse made from fresh ricotta is a common dessert in Southern Italy. While I have enjoyed many charming versions, this simple one from Agriturismo Terre del Principe near Caserta remains my favorite. Well sated by the owner Manuela's dinner, I'd planned to take just one polite bite of her dessert. There was no turning back—after spooning up the last of the rich mousse, I asked Manuela if I might include her recipe in my book. As is typical, she had no written recipe. "It's just ricotta and *mosto cotto*," she told me. Truly, this simple dessert relies only on good, fresh ricotta and a syrup made from grape must or wine, topped with bits of dark chocolate. *Mosto cotto* is easy to make and well worth having on hand. It can also be purchased online (see Sources, page 203).

2 cups (454 g) fresh ricotta (page 186), well drained

6 tablespoons (90 ml) mosto cotto, homemade (page 197) or store-bought, plus more for drizzling

About 2 ounces (56 g) dark chocolate (55 to 70 percent cacao), chopped medium-fine, for serving

Press the ricotta through an ultrafine-mesh strainer or splatter screen (see page 14) into a bowl. Add the *mosto cotto* and beat with a hand-held electric mixer at medium speed until the mixture is fluffy and holds medium-firm peaks, like whipped cream.

Divide the mousse equally among six small dessert cups. Cover with plastic wrap and refrigerate for at least 4 hours, or overnight, to set the mousse.

To serve, sprinkle the tops with chopped chocolate and drizzle with additional *mosto cotto*.

Zabaione al Limoncello con Fragole
strawberries with limoncello sabayon

SERVES 6 | GLUTEN FREE

The sweet, fluffy egg foam known as *zabaione* and popular throughout Italy is most commonly made with Marsala wine. Some Italians replace the wine with liqueur, or even Prosecco. I've made it with nocino (walnut liqueur) and with my homemade limoncello when I've found myself with an abundant supply of it. This sweet-tart, lemony *zabaione* is wonderful dolloped over juicy strawberries or other fruits, such as blackberries, raspberries, nectarines, figs, or a combination. (You can also freeze the *zabaione* mixture in an ice cream maker following the manufacturer's directions for a refreshing gelato.)

To make the dessert in advance, make the *zabaione* a day ahead and refrigerate it overnight in an airtight container. The strawberries should not be prepared more than an hour before serving.

MACERATED STRAWBERRIES

1 pint (175 g) ripe strawberries, hulled and sliced

¹/₄ cup (60 ml) limoncello, homemade (page 200) or store-bought

2 tablespoons sugar, or more to taste

ZABAIONE

4 large egg yolks

Finely grated zest of 1 lemon

¹/₄ cup (50 g) sugar

¹/₂ cup (120 ml) limoncello, homemade (page 200) or store-bought

¹/₂ cup (120 ml) heavy cream

To prepare the strawberries, gently stir the strawberries with the limoncello and sugar to coat them, adding more sugar to taste if the berries are tart. Let the berries stand at room temperature for 1 hour while you make the *zabaione*.

To make the *zabaione*, in the top of a double boiler or in a stainless steel bowl, whisk the egg yolks, lemon zest, and sugar until pale yellow and creamy.

Set the bowl over a pot holding about 1 inch of simmering water over low heat; the bottom of the bowl should not touch the water. Stir in the limoncello. Keeping the water just below a simmer, whisk constantly to keep the *zabaione* constantly in motion until it foams and thickens to the texture of soft pastry cream, 5 to 6 minutes. (It will thicken further as it cools.)

Fill a slightly larger bowl with ice and water, then set the bowl with the *zabaione* over it and stir occasionally until the *zabaione* is completely cool, about 30 minutes, taking care not to slosh water into the bowl.

To serve, whip the cream using an electric mixer until firm peaks form. Use a large spatula to fold the cream into the cooled *zabaione*. Divide the strawberries and their juices among six dessert bowls. Top each with a large dollop of *zabaione*, and serve immediately.

Sfogliatelle Frolle Neapolitan pastry with a semolina and ricotta filling

In Naples you will find two pastries called *sfogliatelle—Sfogliatelle Ricce* (page 101), made with layers of flaky pastry similar to a strudel (and just as challenging to manage), and this easier version, encased in the short-crust pastry known as *pasta frolla*.

The pastries can be prepared and filled a day ahead, refrigerated, and then baked in the morning to enjoy them the way Southern Italians do—as a warm breakfast sweet. They can also be frozen for up to 2 weeks before baking: Arrange the *sfogliatelle* on a parchment paper–lined baking sheet and freeze. Once frozen, wrap the *sfogliatelle* in parchment paper and transfer to a ziplock bag or airtight container and freeze until needed. To enjoy warm *sfogliatelle,* transfer as many as you wish to a parchment paper–lined baking sheet and thaw overnight in the refrigerator. Once the pastries are thawed, transfer the baking sheet to a preheated oven and bake as below.

Short-crust pastry (page 183, single crust)

1 cup (240 ml) whole milk

Pinch of kosher salt

6 tablespoons (65 g) semolina

¹/₂ cup (114 g) fresh ricotta (page 186), well drained

6 tablespoons (75 g) granulated sugar

¹/₄ cup (50 g) packed minced candied orange peel (page 193)

¹/₄ teaspoon pure vanilla extract

¹/₈ teaspoon ground cinnamon

2 large egg yolks

Confectioners' sugar, for dusting

Make the pastry dough, flatten into a disk, wrap in plastic wrap, and chill for at least 1 hour.

Bring the milk and salt to a boil in a small saucepan over medium heat. Remove from the heat and add the semolina in a steady stream as you stir constantly with a whisk to discourage lumps from forming. Return the saucepan to medium heat and cook, stirring constantly, first with the whisk and then with a wooden spoon as the mixture thickens. Continue cooking and stirring until the semolina has the texture of a thick paste, about 2 minutes. Transfer to a bowl and set aside to cool slightly.

While the semolina cools, press the ricotta through an ultrafine-mesh strainer or splatter screen (page 14) into a medium bowl. Mix in the granulated sugar, candied orange peel, vanilla, cinnamon, and 1 of the egg yolks until well blended. Stir in the semolina with a spatula until completely combined, pressing out any lumps against the side of the bowl. Refrigerate until ready to use.

Preheat the oven to 350°F (177°C) with racks in the upper and lower thirds of the oven. Line two baking sheets with silicone baking mats or parchment paper and a third one with plastic wrap.

Roll the pastry between two sheets of plastic wrap to a thickness of about ¹/₄ inch. Use a cutter or overturned small bowl to cut out 4-inch rounds, rerolling the scraps to make a total of ten rounds. Leaving one dough round out, transfer the remaining dough rounds to the baking sheet lined with plastic wrap and refrigerate.

Roll the dough round between two sheets of plastic wrap, rolling away and toward you but not side to side, to form an elongated oval

that measures about $4^{1}/_{2}$ by 6 inches, With a short side facing you, mound 3 tablespoons of the filling near the center of the oval. Using the plastic wrap as a guide, pull the far end toward you, up and over the filling, to fold the pastry in half and enclose the filling. Press the top pastry to the bottom all around the edge to seal. For the prettiest finish, trim the edge with a fluted pastry cutter. Continue to fill and form the remaining pastries, placing them onto the parchment-lined baking sheets as you make them, leaving at least an inch between them. Refrigerate the *sfogliatelle* on the baking sheets as you form them.

Just before baking, whisk the remaining egg yolk lightly in a small bowl and brush it over the tops of the pastries. Bake until golden, 25 to 30 minutes. Let cool for 15 minutes, then serve warm with a dusting of confectioners' sugar.

ABOUT SEMOLINA

Semolina is made by removing the coarse bran and germ from wheat, then milling the remaining endosperm to a sandy texture similar to fine cornmeal. Italians use the ivory-colored grain in cereals, puddings, and desserts. They also grind it finely to make semola, a flour prized for the texture it lends to breads and pastas.

Sfogliatelle Ricce flaky pastries with a semolina and ricotta filling

Sfogliatelle Ricce has been my favorite breakfast pastry as far back as I can remember. Growing up, I had no idea that they originated in Naples because we had them at our local pastry shop in Verbicaro (Calabria). It turns out that the shop's owner was originally from Campania and brought her recipe with her when she married someone from my town.

Sfogliatelle are best eaten warm, the layers of flaky pastry crackling into a million shards as you take a bite. This version of the pastry is called *ricce,* or curly, for those staggered layers of paper-thin pastry, which give the pastry its characteristically appealing look. *Sfogliatelle Frolle* (page 98) are encased in short-crust pastry.

Of the two types of *sfogliatelle, ricce* and *frolle,* these are the more labor-intensive, but the reward is well worth the effort. I must admit that making this type of *sfogliatelle* was something I believed was beyond my ability. But after visiting many pastry shops and experimenting with recipes, I have developed a technique that uses a pasta machine, which is far easier than pulling the dough into thin sheets as they do in pastry shops. The industrial ones made by machine don't hold a candle to these.

Neapolitans will tell you that the only *sfogliatelle* worth their salt are made with *strutto* (lard), but after making them both with lard and with clarified butter, I was surprised by how much I liked the buttery ones. Still, tradition and taste favor the use of lard. If you cannot find pure, nonhydrogenated lard—the type free of chemicals that must be refrigerated—and you do not wish to render your own, clarified butter works quite well.

DOUGH

- 4 cups (528 g) all-purpose flour
- 1 tablespoon plus 1 teaspoon mild-flavored honey, such as clover or orange blossom
- 1 teaspoon kosher salt
- 1 cup (240 ml) water
- 1¹/₄ cups (284 g) pure, nonhydrogenated lard (see headnote) or clarified unsalted butter, melted and cooled to room temperature, plus a bit of softened lard or butter for coating the dough

To make the dough, mix the flour, honey, salt, and water in a stand mixer with the paddle attachment at medium-low speed. Continue to mix at medium speed for 2 minutes after the ingredients come together to form a stiff dough. Transfer the dough to a flat surface and knead by hand for a few minutes to bring the dough together as much as possible. Form the dough into a ball, rub the surface all over with softened lard, and wrap tightly in plastic wrap. Refrigerate for 2 to 4 hours to hydrate the dough and relax the gluten.

Cut the dough into eight equal pieces. Keep the remaining pieces covered in the refrigerator as you work with each one. Flatten or roll one piece of dough into a rectangle a bit narrower than your pasta machine, about 4 inches by 5 inches. Run the dough through the pasta machine twice at each setting, moving from wide to narrow, until you have run it twice through the narrowest one. (A helper is useful here to guide the dough through the machine or catch it as it emerges.)

INGREDIENTS AND METHOD CONTINUED

FILLING

2 cups (480 ml) whole milk

¹/₄ teaspoon kosher salt

³/₄ cup (130 g) semolina

1 cup (227 g) fresh ricotta (page 186), well drained

³/₄ cup (150 g) granulated sugar

2 large egg yolks

¹/₂ cup loosely packed (85 g) minced candied orange peel (page 193)

¹/₂ teaspoon pure vanilla extract

¹/₄ teaspoon ground cinnamon

Confectioners' sugar, for dusting

Lay the dough on a smooth, flat table or counter top that is at least 6 feet long and 14 inches wide. Taking care not to tear the dough more than necessary (a couple of small tears won't matter), and working in manageable sections, anchor the dough on the long side by pressing one edge against the work surface while gently stretching and pulling from the opposite edge of the dough until the entire length of the dough is 12 to 14 inches wide and a bit longer than when you started. The dough should be so thin you can nearly see through it.

Brush the dough with the melted lard, warming it just slightly if needed. Starting at one of the narrow ends, begin to roll the dough into a tight log, pulling gently as you roll to stretch the dough even thinner, and stopping when there are a few inches remaining, which you will use to overlap with the next piece of dough. Repeat with each of the remaining pieces of dough, overlapping the ends of the new and old sheets to create a single tight roll about 2 inches in diameter. Trim the ends with

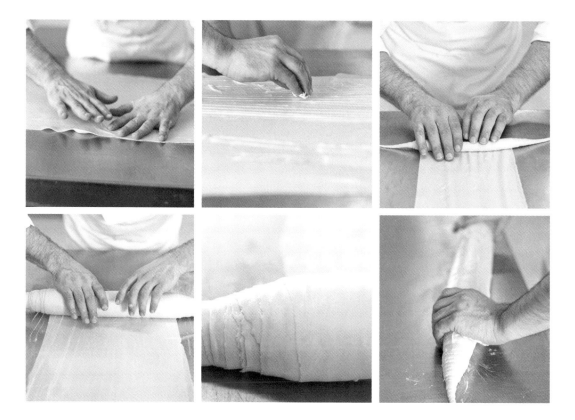

a sharp knife to make a 12-inch log. Rub the surface all over with lard or butter, wrap tightly in plastic wrap, and refrigerate for 8 to 24 hours. (The dough can be wrapped once in plastic wrap and again in aluminum foil and frozen for up to 2 weeks; thaw overnight in the refrigerator.)

To make the filling, bring the milk and salt to a boil in a small saucepan over medium heat. Remove from the heat and add the semolina in a steady stream as you stir constantly with a whisk to discourage lumps from forming. Return the saucepan to medium heat and cook, stirring constantly, first with the whisk and then with a wooden spoon. Continue cooking and stirring as the mixture thickens, until the semolina has the texture of a thick paste, about 2 minutes. Transfer to a bowl and set aside to cool slightly.

While the semolina cools, press the ricotta through an ultrafine-mesh strainer or splatter screen (page 14) into a medium bowl. Mix in the sugar, egg yolks, candied orange peel, vanilla, and cinnamon until well blended. Stir in the semolina with a spatula until completely combined, pressing out any lumps against the side of the bowl. Refrigerate until ready to use.

Preheat the oven to 425°F (218°C) with racks in the upper and lower thirds of the oven. Line two baking sheets with parchment paper or silicone baking mats. Cut the pastry roll into 1/2-inch-thick slices.

CONTINUED

There are two methods for forming the *sfogliatelle:* entirely by hand, or using a rolling pin or tortilla press—certainly not a traditional method in Italy!

Method #1: Working with one slice at a time, use your thumbs and middle fingers to shape the dough. Hold a dough slice flat in your two hands, palms facing up, with the tips of your first two fingers supporting the dough on the underside and your thumbs on top. Continually rotate the slice between your fingers as you use your thumbs to gently push the dough from the center outward toward the edges to enlarge the circle by separating out the layers of dough. You don't want to separate the ribs completely; rather you are seeking to slide them apart. When the disk is about 4 inches in diameter, use your thumbs and fingers to shape it into a bell shape with the opening at the bottom, as you continue to turn it between your fingers. It may help to think of the technique as similar to opening a collapsible drinking cup.

Method #2: I've devised a second method that is easier and makes slightly shorter, broader *sfogliatelle.* Roll the dough slice between two sheets of plastic wrap, applying equal pressure in each direction, to make a $4^{1}/_{2}$-inch round. Alternatively, if you have a tortilla press, place the dough between two sheets of plastic wrap, place on the press, and press down firmly on the handle to flatten the dough. A good, strong press will do the job, but if it is not quite wide enough, you can finish it with a rolling pin. Fold the dough round to form a bell shape that is open at the bottom.

Whichever method you used to form the shell, continue to shape the remaining dough slices in the same manner. Pick up a *sfogliatella* shell and fill it with $2^{1}/_{2}$ tablespoons of the filling, then mold it into a clam shape, pressing to close and seal the bottom. Continue to fill the remaining *sfogliatelle*, placing them about two inches apart on the prepared baking sheets as you form them.

Bake for 5 minutes, then decrease the heat to 400°F (204°C) and bake until golden, about 25 minutes longer.

Serve warm, dusted with confectioners' sugar. Leftover *sfogliatelle* may be refrigerated for up to 3 days; warm them in a toaster oven before serving.

Zeppole di San Giuseppe Saint Joseph's fried pastries

March 19 commemorates Saint Joseph's Day, honoring the father of Jesus and celebrated throughout Italy as Father's Day. Each region has its own dessert for the occasion, and in many parts of Southern Italy, these Neapolitan pastries topped with pastry cream and an amarena cherry are the treat of choice. The pastry is formed in a round doughnut shape, but the batter is similar to the French pâte à choux, used to make cream puffs and eclairs. The same batter is used in Palermo's Sfince di San Giuseppe (page 58), celebrating the same holiday. There, the dough is fried in round puffs and filled with ricotta cream.

To bake rather than fry the *zeppole*, pipe the dough in rings on a parchment paper–lined baking sheet and bake in a preheated 400°F (204°C) oven for about 25 minutes, until golden. Fill and serve as below.

BATTER

1 cup (240 ml) water

$^1/_2$ cup (113 g) unsalted butter

Pinch of kosher salt

1$^3/_4$ cups (230 g) all-purpose flour

7 large eggs

Vegetable oil, for frying

FILLING

1$^1/_8$ cups (320 g) pastry cream (page 185), made with 2 additional egg yolks (4 total)

18 preserved amarena cherries, for garnish

To make the batter, combine the water, butter, and salt in a saucepan and bring to a boil. Turn off the heat and add the flour all at once. Turn the heat to low and cook, stirring and pressing the dough with a wooden spoon, until all of the flour is absorbed and the dough pulls away from the sides and bottom of the pan. Continue to cook and stir for 1 minute longer to cook off the raw flour taste.

Transfer the dough to the bowl of a stand mixer fitted with the paddle attachment. At low speed, add the eggs, one at a time, mixing until each egg is well incorporated before adding the next. The batter will be thick.

Heat 3 inches of oil to 350°F (177°C) in a deep pot or fryer. Fit a pastry bag with a $^7/_{16}$-inch star tip, such as Ateco #825. Line a baking sheet with paper towels.

Lay out sheets of parchment paper on a flat surface and, using a 3-inch round cutter or inverted glass as a guide, draw eighteen circles on the parchment paper with a pencil, leaving about 2 inches between them. Turn over the parchment paper so that the writing can be seen through it, and pipe rings of dough onto the parchment paper, using the circles as a guide. Cut between the rings with scissors to separate each *zeppole* onto its own piece of parchment paper.

To fry the *zeppole*, carefully slip a ring on its parchment paper into the hot oil, adjusting the heat to maintain it at 350°F (177°C). Use tongs to pull the parchment paper from the oil as it separates from the

CONTINUED

zeppole; set aside to cool and discard. Drop in a second ring and again retrieve the parchment paper. Use the tongs to continually turn the *zeppole* as they puff and brown, about 4 minutes. Allow the oil to drip back into the pot before transferring the *zeppole* to the paper towel–lined baking sheet as they are done. Continue to add the rings, pull off the parchment paper, turn, and brown the *zeppole* until you have fried them all. Cool just until they can be easily handled.

Use the pastry bag fitted with the star tip, or a spoon, to cover the small hole in the center of each *zeppole* with pastry cream. (The pastry ring will puff and nearly close as it fries.) Top each with an amarena cherry and serve warm.

La Coviglia al Caffè frozen espresso mousse

SERVES 6 TO 9 | GLUTEN FREE

This classic *semifreddo*, or half-frozen dessert, is found in Neapolitan ice cream shops. At one time it was served in small bell-shaped aluminum cups called *coviglie*. Nowadays, it is more often found in clear plastic cups of the same shape, topped with a clear lid. Always made in a single flavor, classic varieties include chocolate, hazelnut, strawberry, and this one—coffee. I first tried this simple yet luscious dessert at Caffè Gambrinus in the heart of Naples, where they have been making *coviglia* since the late 1800s, when fashionable ladies sat at the cafe tables enjoying small cups of this rich dessert.

If you have scraps of sponge cake or *savoiardi* (lady's fingers) available, follow the traditional Neapolitan way of serving these: place a small piece of cake in the bottom of each cup and drizzle with a teaspoon or two of liqueur before filling with the mousse. Small espresso or demitasse cups are the perfect vessel, but you can use ramekins or other dishes with 1/3- to 1/2-cup capacity.

2 large eggs, separated

1/2 cup (100 g) sugar

1/4 cup freshly made espresso, or 1 tablespoon instant espresso granules dissolved in 1/4 cup (60 ml) hot water

Pinch of kosher salt

3/4 cup (180 ml) heavy cream

6 to 9 chocolate-covered espresso beans, for garnish (optional)

Beat the egg yolks with 1/4 cup of the sugar in a metal bowl with a handheld electric mixture at high speed until light, about 1 minute. Add the espresso, then whisk the mixture over, but not touching, simmering water in a small saucepan until it is thick and creamy, like a cream sauce, 3 to 4 minutes. The temperature should reach about 175°F (79°C). Remove the bowl from the heat and refrigerate until cool, about 15 minutes. (To speed cooling, set the bowl over a bowl of ice and water and let cool, stirring frequently, taking care not to slosh water into the coffee mixture.)

While the coffee mixture cools, beat the egg whites with the salt at high speed until foamy. Gradually add the remaining 1/4 cup of sugar, 1 tablespoon at a time, and continue beating until firm, shiny peaks form.

In a separate bowl, whip the cream using an electric mixer until firm peaks form. Stir the completely cooled coffee mixture, then use a large spatula to gently fold in the whipped cream. Finally, fold in the egg whites until completely blended, taking care not to deflate the mousse.

Pour the mousse into small espresso cups or ramekins, filling each with 1/3 to 1/2 cup of mousse. Cover with plastic wrap and freeze until firm, at least 2 hours or up to 1 week. If they have frozen hard, let stand at room temperature for about 10 minutes, until it has the texture of a semi-frozen mousse. Top each with a chocolate-covered espresso bean, if using, and serve.

Gelato ai Cachi persimmon ice cream

MAKES ABOUT 1 QUART (1 L) | GLUTEN FREE

This gelato conveys the essence of persimmon. Use very ripe fruit—it should look almost translucent, as if it were a water balloon about to burst. The liqueur helps to keep the ice cream soft and creamy and adds a typical Southern Italian flavor that complements the fruit. If you find yourself with extra persimmon purée, stir in a few drops of lemon juice and drizzle as a sauce over the gelato.

1^1/$_2$ pounds (680 g) very ripe Hachiya persimmons (5 to 6 medium)

1 cup (240 ml) whole milk

1 cup (240 ml) heavy cream

^{1}/$_2$ cup (100 g) sugar

2 tablespoons Strega liqueur

Remove the calyx (the leafy part where the stem attaches) from the persimmons with a paring knife, as you would the stem of a strawberry or tomato. Use a large spoon to scoop the flesh into a strainer set over a bowl or large measuring cup, drawing the spoon closely against the skin to remove as much of the flesh as possible. (Discard any dark parts or pits.) Press the persimmon through the strainer until only a few stubborn pieces remain in the strainer—enjoy these as a snack or discard. Set aside 1^1/$_2$ cups of the purée; reserve any remaining purée for another use.

Heat the milk, cream, and sugar in a saucepan, stirring over medium heat just long enough to dissolve the sugar. The mixture should not be hot. Stir in the Strega and the persimmon purée.

Refrigerate the mixture until it is very cold, about 4 hours. (To speed cooling, set the bowl inside a larger bowl filled with ice and water, stirring occasionally until cold, taking care not to slosh water into the mixture.) Freeze the mixture in an ice cream machine according to the manufacturer's directions.

Transfer the gelato to an airtight container and freeze until firm, 2 to 3 hours, before serving.

3

Calabria

Having been born and raised in Calabria, I must admit to the biased opinion that it is the best spot in all of Southern Italy. This southernmost area marking the toe of the Italian boot is off the tourist path for most, so its lifestyles and traditions have remained largely unknown. It is a lush area with a diverse geography offering mountain pastures, dense forests, terraced vineyards, and vast groves of fragrant citrus. Aside from the Pollino Mountains to the north, separating Calabria from Basilicata, we face water on all sides, with coastlines on the Tyrrhenian and Ionian Seas and the Strait of Messina.

As in all Southern Italian regions, Calabrian sweets reflect the Greek, Roman, Byzantine, Norman, and Spanish conquerors who have at one time or another ruled the area, bringing with them their most favored ingredients and traditions. Desserts here are heavily influenced by the region's proximity to Campania and Sicily. Yet, beyond the common ingredients found throughout Southern Italy, Calabria enjoys many specialties not found in the other regions: citron and bergamot, abundant figs,

chestnuts, and licorice root. Even our hot Calabrian peppers occasionally find their way into desserts, such as the sweet-spicy Crostata del Diavolo (page 124).

The small town of Verbicaro was my home until I came to the United States at the age of fourteen. In my younger years I rarely encountered homemade desserts; we had little kitchen equipment, no great supply of baking ingredients, and only our wood-burning oven used for breads and savory dishes. Cattle were not used for milk—our dairy supply came from goats and sheep, whose milk was transformed into cheeses, and the whey that remained from cheese making was made into *ricotta fresca* (page 186). We kept chickens, but their eggs weren't meant to be squandered on pastry, but rather were saved to fortify our meals. What ingredients we did use we mostly grew or made ourselves. Our trees grew my favored Dottato figs. Our olive trees produced exquisite oil. We candied aromatic citron to make *cedro candito*. The grapes on our vines were transformed not only into wine, but also into the concentrated grape must syrup called *mosto cotto* (page 197).

My mother, who taught me the secrets of the kitchen, had even less to work with: she was raised at a time when sugar was a rare commodity, scarce and dear. When they were made at all, desserts were sweetened with homemade syrups like *mosto cotto* (page 197), *miele di fichi* (page 198), or local honey, still found in traditional Calabrian desserts today. Yet, despite having no training and scant equipment and ingredients, she was able to miraculously turn out light, eggy *Pan di Spagna* (page 184) for my birthday as we tiptoed around, trying not to cause it to fall.

More typically, dessert in my childhood home was whatever fruit was in season, or fruits from our trees dried to preserve them, or plain cookies. Home bakers made most of their desserts using some combination of the local dried figs, raisins, chestnuts, almonds, walnuts, ricotta, citrus, wines, and homemade liqueurs, combined with flour and olive oil, and enriched with *strutto* (lard). The local wild fennel and black anise seeds were also popular flavorings. Simple desserts were often made by shaping and frying dough, as was typical in other parts of Southern Italy before the advent of the modern oven. *Mosto cotto*

or honey remained the sweeteners of choice. I still enjoy *mosto cotto* with pecorino cheese and pears for a simple dessert, and either the grape must syrup or *miele di fichi* drizzled over ice cream or homemade ricotta.

When a *pasticceria* opened in my town, I quickly began to spend my pocket money purchasing treats there. I could rarely pass by, morning or afternoon, without stopping in for a bombolone, my favorite cream-filled doughnut, or a *sfogliatella* (page 101). By this time, in the late 1950s, homes and pastry shops were finally equipped with refrigerators and ovens. The transport of ingredients from other regions meant that pastries once found only in Campania and Sicily now lined the shelves of Calabrian pastry shops, enriched with dairy, chocolate, and granulated sugar, all previously unknown in my hometown.

For the most part, desserts were reserved for special occasions like baptisms, communions, or weddings, or for a saint's day; even then, they were meant to be more symbolic than indulgent. For Carnevale, Calabrians chat with family and friends over plates of just-fried, sugar-dusted *chiacchiere* (page 117). At Easter, sweet breads similar to those found throughout Southern Italy are decorated with hard-cooked eggs to celebrate spring, rebirth, and resurrection. Their names vary by region, and include *buccellati*, *cuzzupe*, and *cuddure*. Also found at that time is the traditional Neapolitan *pastiera*. In summer, each town honors its patron saint with a *festa,* or celebration, including a parade through the streets followed by feasting and sweets. Throughout December, tables are piled high with fritters, cakes, confections, and cookies of all kinds in celebration of the winter holidays, beginning with the *cuccia* (wheat berry pudding) marking the feast of Santa Lucia. A popular cookie is the ladder-shaped *scalille* (also called *scalidde*), which signifies the climb to the heavens. I've left out many of the traditional Calabrian holiday desserts already included in my previous book, *My Calabria,* instead focusing on my personal favorites and those for which I could find no existing documentation. In that book you will find the ricotta-filled, fried ravioli called *chinulille,* a similar fried ravioli called *chinule* filled with chestnut paste and glazed with honey, and *pitta 'mpigliata,* pastry rosettes filled with nuts, raisins, and cinnamon, topped with honey.

As do Italy's other regions, each of Calabria's provinces has its own specialties. In Reggio Calabria, the region's southernmost point, *petrali* are filled with a combination of dried figs, nuts, chocolate, *mosto cotto*, orange peel, and candied citron, then painted with a glaze of white or dark chocolate. *Pignolata* are small fritters glazed with lemon or chocolate, similar to the ones found in Messina, Sicily. Similar to *struffoli,* the fritters called *cicirata* are coated with honey. Reggio Calabria is the only Calabrian town where you will find locals enjoying a scoop of gelato tucked into a brioche for breakfast, as they do in Palermo; Reggio claims it as their own tradition.

Chiacchiere sugar-dusted fried pastry strips

Chiacchiere means chatter, chit-chat, or gossip, and these crispy fried pastry strips dusted with confectioners' sugar are just the thing to nibble on as you talk. Sugar-coated fried pastry is popular throughout Italy and goes by many regional names, including *bugie, cenci, crostoli,* and *frappe.* Enjoy these the day they are made. *Chiacchere* always show up on the Calabrian table for Carnevale.

2^1/$_2$ cups (330 g) all-purpose flour

^{1}/$_2$ teaspoon baking powder

^{1}/$_4$ cup (57 g) unsalted butter, melted and cooled

1 large egg, at room temperature

6 tablespoons (90 ml) white wine

2 tablespoons light rum or anisette

1 tablespoon granulated sugar

1 teaspoon pure vanilla extract

Vegetable oil, for frying

Confectioners' sugar, for dusting

Whisk together the flour and baking powder in a bowl. Set aside.

In a large bowl, use a fork to mix the melted butter, egg, wine, rum, granulated sugar, and vanilla until well blended. Add the flour mixture, 1 cup at a time, until well blended. Briefly knead the dough in the bowl with one hand until smooth and just a little bit sticky. Cover the bowl and refrigerate for 30 minutes.

Divide the chilled dough into quarters. Flatten one quarter and run it through a pasta machine, beginning at the widest setting and continuing twice through each setting, until the dough is about ^{1}/$_{16}$-inch thick. (Alternatively, use a rolling pin to roll the dough to a thickness of ^{1}/$_{16}$ inch.)

With a fluted pastry cutter, cut the dough crosswise into 5- to 6-inch segments, then cut each segment in the opposite direction into 1-inch strips. Cut a 2-inch slit lengthwise down the center of each strip. Pick up a strip, insert one end of the dough through the slit and thread it all the way through to form a twist at the center. Repeat with the remaining pastry strips.

Heat 4 inches of oil to 375°F (190°C) in a heavy 6-quart pot over medium-high heat. Line a tray with paper towels.

Use a metal skimmer or large slotted spoon to carefully transfer the strips, a few at a time, into the hot oil, taking care not to crowd them. The *chiacchiere* will puff immediately. Use the skimmer or spoon to keep them moving in the oil until they are golden all over, 1 to 2 minutes.

As they are done, allow the oil to drip back into the pot before transferring the *chiacchiere* to the prepared tray to drain briefly, then transfer them to a serving platter. Continue to fry the *chiacchiere*, dusting them generously with confectioners' sugar while still warm as you transfer them to the platter. Let cool for a few minutes before serving.

Biscotti di Zia Flora Aunt Flora's lemon-glazed cookies

To help relieve our homesick feelings when we first moved to Oakland in 1974, my Aunt Flora taught my mother to make these lemony wreath-shaped cookies. Zia Flora always seemed to have a plate of them ready to serve in her home, or with her to share with friends. I have seen the popular cookie called by other names: *ginetti,* Italian lemon cookies, *biscotti con la glassa al limone,* and *taralli con glassa.* Because we associate them with my Zia Flora, Biscotti di Zia Flora is what we call them in my home.

I've tried making these in my stand mixer, but I think they turn out better when made by my mother's low-tech method, using only a bowl, a fork, and hands. The recipe can be doubled easily for holiday cookie making. The finished cookies can be stored in an airtight container with parchment paper separating the layers for up to 2 weeks, or frozen in ziplock bags for up to a month; thaw in the bag at room temperature.

2 large eggs

$^1/_4$ cup (57 g) unsalted butter, melted and cooled to room temperature

$^1/_4$ cup (50 g) granulated sugar

1 teaspoon finely grated lemon zest

1 tablespoon fresh lemon juice

1 tablespoon 2 percent or whole milk

$^1/_2$ teaspoon pure vanilla extract

1 teaspoon baking powder

2 cups (264 g) all-purpose flour, plus more for rolling

GLAZE

1 cup (125 g) confectioners' sugar

Up to 3 tablespoons (45 ml) fresh lemon juice

Rainbow diavoletti (sprinkles) (optional)

Crack the eggs into a mixing bowl and whisk with a fork to break them up. Stir in the butter, sugar, lemon zest and juice, milk, and vanilla. Stir the baking powder into the flour and add to the egg mixture, continuing to stir with the fork until all of the flour is incorporated. Finish mixing by kneading the dough with your hands in the bowl to make a smooth dough. Cover the bowl and refrigerate until the dough is firm, 1 to 2 hours.

When you are ready to form the cookies, preheat the oven to 375°F (190℃) with a rack in the center of the oven. Line a baking sheet with parchment paper or a silicone baking mat.

To form the cookies, divide the dough into twenty-four approximately equal pieces. Roll each piece with your hands on a flat surface to form a rope about 9 inches long and $^3/_8$ inch diameter, using a bit of flour only if the dough sticks. Fold the rope in half to form a double strand, pressing the two ends together. Then, hold one end of the doubled rope while twisting the other end to form a twist. Connect the two ends to form a ring and pinch closed where they meet. Place the cookie on the prepared baking sheet. Repeat to make twenty-four wreaths, spacing them evenly on the sheet with at least $^1/_2$ inch between them.

Bake the cookies until they are golden on the bottom and firm, about 20 minutes. The tops will not color much. Transfer the baking sheet to a rack to cool completely.

To make the glaze, put the confectioners' sugar in a bowl and stir in 2 tablespoons of lemon juice until smooth. Stir in additional lemon juice, a little bit at a time, to make a glaze the texture of thick cream.

Place the cooled cookies on a rack set over a baking sheet. Pick up a cookie and dunk the top side into the glaze, then hold it over the bowl to let the excess drip off. Place the cookie back on the rack. Continue to glaze the remaining cookies. If using *diavoletti,* sprinkle them over the cookies as you make them, while the glaze is still soft. Let the cookies stand until the glaze dries, at least 1 hour, before serving or packing into containers.

Bocconotti tartlets with three fillings

These rich tartlets originated in the Calabrian town of Mormanno, where they are filled with grape jam or cherry preserves. Families throughout Southern Italy have their own versions. The cookies might be spiced with cinnamon and cloves for Christmas or simply filled with jam. In Basilicata, you will find them filled with *conserva di amarene* (sour cherry preserves); through-out Puglia, they are filled with almond paste or with pastry cream and *amarene*. In Bitonto (Puglia), *bocconotti* are filled with ricotta and candied orange.

When someone wrote asking me about a family version filled with chocolate and almonds, I had to find a recipe. The one I found came from the town of Amantea, and it is the only version I've seen that is left open, with no pastry on top.

I prefer the small *bocconotti* made in 2³/₄ inch (measured across the top) fluted brioche molds, but most *bocconotti* use a larger mold of about 3¹/₂ inches in diameter, which yield only half as many tartlets. (These larger bocconotti will take 10 to 15 minutes longer to bake.) I've included my three favorite variations here. For the amarena cherries in syrup, look for Toschi or Fabbri brands.

Short-crust pastry (page 183, single crust for open bocconotti or double crust for covered)

Filling (choose from the filling recipes that follow)

Confectioners' sugar, for finishing

Prepare the pastry dough, flatten it into a disk, wrap in plastic wrap, and chill for at least 1 hour.

Preheat the oven to 375°F (190°C) with a rack in the center of the oven.

To make open-top *bocconotti*: Shape the single crust recipe of pastry dough into a square and divide the square into quarters, then cut each quarter in quarters again to make sixteen pieces. Press one piece evenly into each 2³/₄ inch tartlet mold, molding it firmly against the bottom and up the sides in an even layer. Trim away any excess dough from around the edges.

To make covered *bocconotti*: Shape the double crust recipe of pastry dough into a square and divide the square into quarters, then cut each quarter into quarters again to make sixteen pieces. Pinch off about one-third of each piece to use for the tops, flattening them into 2-inch rounds on a piece of plastic wrap. Press each of the larger pieces evenly into a 2³/₄ inch tartlet mold, pressing it firmly against the bottom and up the sides in an even layer. (Do not trim.)

Fill the tartlets with one of the fillings below, using a rounded tablespoon for each. If making covered tarts, use a small offset spatula to place the tops over the filling, pinching the tops and bottoms together all around the edges to seal them.

CONTINUED

Space the filled tartlets evenly on a baking sheet. Bake until the centers puff and crack and the crust is golden, about 20 minutes for open tarts and 25 for closed.

Transfer the tartlets in their molds to a rack to cool. When cool enough to handle, pop the *bocconotti* from the molds and let them cool directly on the rack. Dust with confectioners' sugar just before serving.

Chocolate Almond Filling

Use this filling to make open-top Bocconotti Calabrese.

¹/₂ cup (75 g) skin-on almonds

2 ounces (57 g) semisweet or dark chocolate (55 to 70 percent cacao), coarsely chopped

¹/₄ cup (50 g) sugar

2 tablespoons unsweetened cocoa powder, preferably Dutch-processed

¹/₄ teaspoon ground cinnamon

Pinch of ground cloves

2 large egg whites

Pinch of kosher salt

¹/₂ teaspoon pure vanilla extract

Combine the almonds, chocolate, sugar, cocoa, cinnamon, and cloves in a food processor and process until the mixture has the texture of fine bread crumbs. Beat the egg whites with the salt at high speed in a clean bowl with clean beaters until medium-firm peaks form that drape over gently and hold their shape. Use a large spatula to gently fold the almond mixture into the egg whites in four additions, folding until well combined. Fold in the vanilla with the last addition.

Ricotta and Candied Orange Filling

Use this filling to make covered Bocconotti di Bitonto with ricotta and orange.

1 cup (224 g) fresh ricotta (page 186), well drained

1/3 cup (67 g) sugar

2 large eggs, separated

2 tablespoons packed finely chopped (1/4-inch) candied orange peel (page 193)

1/4 teaspoon pure vanilla extract

1/8 teaspoon ground cinnamon (optional)

Press the ricotta through an ultrafine-mesh strainer or splatter screen (see page 14) into a bowl. Use a silicone spatula to stir in the sugar, egg yolks, candied orange peel, vanilla, and cinnamon (if using) until smooth. In a separate bowl, beat the egg whites with an electric mixer at high speed until firm peaks form that are not at all dry. Use a spatula to fold the whites into the ricotta mixture in three additions.

Almond–Amarena Cherry Filling

Use this filling to make covered bocconotti with almond and amarena cherries.

2/3 cup (112 g) blanched almonds (page 189)

1/4 cup (50 g) sugar

2 tablespoons Amaretto di Saronno

1/2 teaspoon pure almond extract

1 large egg white

12 preserved amarena cherries, such as Toschi or Fabbri brand

Combine the almonds and sugar in a food processor and process to a fine meal. Transfer the mixture to a bowl and use a silicone spatula to stir in the amaretto and almond extract to make a thick paste.

In a clean bowl with clean beaters, beat the egg white at high speed until medium-firm peaks form that are not at all dry. Use a large spatula to fold one-third of the egg whites into the almond mixture to loosen it, then fold in the remaining whites in two parts until well combined.

When filling the tarts, tuck a cherry into the middle of each.

Crostata del Diavolo sweet and spicy pepper tart

This spicy-sweet tart is the creation of Ristorante Sabbia d'Oro, located in Belvedere Marittimo, near Diamante, where a festival celebrating the area's famed hot peppers fills the streets with devilishly good food each September. Calabrians use their local hot peppers in anything and everything, often pairing them with cheese and here mixing pepper jam with orange marmalade to temper the heat in this addictive dessert. Look for imported Calabrian *confettura* or *marmellata di peperoncini* for the best, most authentic jam (see Sources, page 203), or purchase a sweet-hot red pepper jam (not jelly).

Short-crust pastry (page 183, double crust)

1/2 cup (57 g) sliced almonds

3/4 cup (255 g) orange marmalade, homemade (page 194) or store-bought

1/3 cup (90 g) confettura di peperoncini (hot red pepper jam)

Confectioners' sugar, for finishing

Make the pastry dough, flatten into a disk, wrap in plastic wrap, and chill for at least 1 hour.

Preheat the oven to 375°F (190°C) with a rack in the center of the oven.

Divide the pastry in two, one piece larger than the other (approximately one-third and two-thirds). Roll the larger piece between two sheets of plastic wrap into an 12-inch round. Peel off the top sheet of plastic, then invert the round over a 9- by 1-inch tart pan with a removable bottom, nestling it to cover the bottom and sides of the pan. Roll the pin over the top to trim the pastry flush with the top of the pan.

On a flat surface, knead the almonds into the smaller piece of pastry, then roll it between two sheets of plastic wrap into a 9-inch round.

Spread the orange marmalade over the pastry in the pan, covering the bottom evenly. Dollop the pepper jam evenly over the marmalade. Top the tart with the 9-inch pastry round, pressing it into the sides of the bottom pastry all around. Gently fold the edges of the bottom pastry down over the top and press all around to seal the top to the sides.

Bake until the pastry is golden, about 30 minutes. Cool completely on a wire rack.

To serve, remove the sides of the pan and place the tart on its base on a serving platter. Dust the crostata generously with confectioners' sugar. Serve at room temperature, cut into wedges.

Torta di Mele e Ricotta apple and ricotta cake

I met Fiorina Mastroianni when she contacted me after reading an article about my Calabrian cooking classes. Now living in Australia, she, too, is originally from Calabria, and she hoped to teach cooking classes in her area. She and I have become fast friends, at least virtually. When she shared her recipe for pear and ricotta cake, I expected it to be similar to the ricotta mousse cake with poached pears popular on the Amalfi Coast. Fiorina's recipe was more cakey than mousse-like, and I liked the addition of ricotta. I substituted apples for pears, and the result is this variation of Fiorina's recipe, which I like very much.

I use the Fuji apples that grow in my backyard. When using apples in place of pears, Fiorina sometimes makes hers with Granny Smiths. Any firm-fleshed, tart-sweet apple will do.

1 cup (227 g) fresh ricotta (page 186), well drained

3 large apples (about 750 g), peeled and cored

2 teaspoons fresh lemon juice

1$^{1}/_{2}$ cups (200 g) all-purpose flour

2 teaspoons baking powder

$^{1}/_{2}$ teaspoon kosher salt

3 large eggs, separated

$^{1}/_{2}$ cup (100 g) granulated sugar

1 teaspoon pure vanilla extract

Finely grated zest of 1 lemon

2 tablespoons coarse sugar, for sprinkling

Preheat the oven to 350°F (177°C) with a rack in the center. Butter and flour a 9- by 2$^{1}/_{2}$-inch springform pan, knocking out any excess flour.

Press the ricotta through an ultrafine-mesh strainer or splatter screen (see page 14) into a bowl. Set aside.

Cut two of the apples into $^{1}/_{2}$-inch dice. Put them in a bowl and toss them with the lemon juice. (The third apple will be used later.)

Stir together the flour, baking powder, and salt in a small bowl. In a clean bowl using a handheld electric mixer and clean beaters, beat the egg whites at high speed until firm peaks form that are not at all dry.

Beat the egg yolks with the granulated sugar in a large bowl with an electric mixer at medium speed until light and creamy, about 1 minute. Add the ricotta, vanilla, and lemon zest and continue to mix at low speed until well blended. Add the flour mixture and mix just until combined. Use a large spatula to fold in the apples, and then the egg whites in three additions.

Spread the batter evenly in the prepared pan. Cut the last apple into thin slices and arrange them in concentric circles over the surface (you may not need them all), pressing them gently into the batter. Sprinkle the coarse sugar generously over the top.

Bake the cake until the top is golden and a skewer tests clean near the center, 75 to 80 minutes. Transfer the pan to a rack to cool completely.

Run a knife around the edge of the cake to loosen it, then remove the sides of the pan. Transfer the cake on its base to a serving platter and serve. Cover leftovers tightly and store at room temperature for up to 1 day, or refrigerate for up to 3 days.

Ciambella all'Arancia orange-scented olive oil cake

SERVES 12

No matter whether it is a bread, cake, or donut, if it is ring-shaped and you can eat it, in Italy we call it *ciambella*. This moist, orange-scented, cake is one of my favorites for coffee or tea time. I was served a similar cake topped with a spoonful of homemade marmalade for breakfast at Casa Janca Agriturismo in Pizzo. My version gets a beautiful shine by soaking the baked cake with orange juice. Chopped candied orange peel gives the cut slices a jeweled appearance.

The standard Italian *ciambella* pan has a diameter of 26 centimeters (about 10 inches) and is 8 centimeters (about 3 inches) high, with a tube in the center that is taller than the sides of the pan. The cake also turns out well when baked in a Bundt or standard tube pan.

Look for oranges that have not been sprayed or waxed because you will be using quite a bit of the rind; you will need about six large oranges. It is easiest to zest the oranges before juicing them.

3 cups (396 g) all-purpose flour

1 tablespoon baking powder

$^1/_2$ teaspoon kosher salt, plus a pinch for the egg whites

4 large eggs, separated

$1^1/_4$ cups plus 2 tablespoons (275 g) sugar

$^3/_4$ cup (180 ml) mild-flavored (buttery) extra-virgin olive oil

3 tablespoons packed finely grated orange zest

2 cups (480 ml) fresh orange juice

2 teaspoons pure orange extract (optional)

$^1/_3$ cup packed (67 g) finely chopped ($^1/_4$-inch) candied orange peel (page 193)

Preheat the oven to 375°F (190°C) with a rack in the center of the oven. Butter and flour a 10-inch (12-cup) *ciambella*, Bundt, or tube pan, knocking out the excess flour.

Stir together the flour, baking powder, and $^1/_2$ teaspoon of the salt in a bowl. In another bowl, whisk together the egg yolks and $1^1/_4$ cups of the sugar until thick. Whisk in the olive oil, orange zest, $1^1/_2$ cups of the orange juice, and the orange extract, if you are using it. Stir in the flour mixture just until it is combined.

Beat the egg whites with a pinch of salt in the bowl of a stand mixer at medium-high speed until medium-firm peaks form that are not at all dry. Use a large spatula to gently fold the egg whites into the batter. Fold in the candied orange peel. Spread the batter evenly in the prepared pan.

Bake until the top of the cake splits and begins to turn golden, about 40 minutes. A toothpick inserted into the cake should come out clean.

Let the cake cool in the pan until you can easily handle it, about 20 minutes. Unmold the cake onto a wire rack top side up and place the rack over a rimmed baking sheet. (When using a *ciambella* pan, the cake is traditionally served split side up.) Let the cake cool completely.

To make the soaking syrup, strain the remaining $^1/_2$ cup of orange juice into a small bowl and stir in the remaining 2 tablespoons of sugar until it dissolves. Slowly pour the syrup evenly over the top of the cake, allowing it to soak in as you pour. Use a pastry brush to brush the remaining syrup all over the outside of the cake.

To serve, cut the cake in slices using a thin, sharp knife or serrated knife. Store leftovers at room temperature, well wrapped, for up to 2 days, or freeze for up to one month.

Torta di Ciliege cherry almond cake

SERVES 10 TO 12 | GLUTEN FREE

This flourless, dairy-free cake is light and moist, with a soft crumb and a layer of cherries at the bottom—perfect for breakfast or tea. I developed the cake from notes I took after tasting a similar cake in Calabria. Alas, when I returned to my notes, I found an ingredient list but nothing else. It took only a few tries to arrive at something quite similar to the cake I remembered. I've made the cake with berries, figs, or peaches in place of the cherries and found the variations equally charming, so feel free to improvise with whatever soft fruits are in season.

1 cup (150 g) blanched almonds (page 189)

3/4 cup (90 g) confectioners' sugar, plus more for finishing

1/2 cup (64 g) potato starch

1 1/2 teaspoons baking powder

4 large eggs, separated

Pinch of kosher salt

1/2 cup (100 g) granulated sugar

1/2 cup (120 ml) mild-flavored (buttery) olive oil

2 tablespoons maraschino liqueur

1/2 teaspoon pure vanilla extract

1/2 teaspoon pure almond extract

Finely grated zest of 1 lemon

16 ounces (454 g) fresh bing or other sweet cherries, pitted

Preheat the oven to 350°F (177°C) with a rack in the center of the oven. Oil or butter a 9-inch round springform pan.

Combine the almonds with the confectioners' sugar in a blender or food processor and process to make a powder almost as fine as flour. Add the potato starch and the baking powder and pulse just a couple of times to combine. Set aside.

In a clean bowl with clean beaters, beat the egg whites and salt in a stand mixer with the whisk attachment at high speed until soft peaks form. Gradually add 1/4 cup of the granulated sugar and continue beating until nearly firm peaks form, slightly curling over when you lift the beater.

Beat the egg yolks with the remaining 1/4 cup of granulated sugar in a stand mixer with the whisk attachment at high speed until they have tripled in volume, about 5 minutes. At low speed, mix in the olive oil, liqueur, vanilla and almond extracts, lemon zest, and the ground almonds.

Use a large spatula to fold one-third of the whites into the yolk and nut mixture to lighten it, then gently fold in the rest of the whites in two additions.

Spread the batter evenly into the prepared pan. Place the cherries evenly over the top of the batter. (The cherries tend to sink as the cake bakes.) Bake until the cake is golden and pulling away from the sides of the pan, about 45 minutes, tenting aluminum foil over the pan for the last 15 minutes or so if the top is browning too quickly. A toothpick will test clean when it is ready (if you avoid hitting a cherry).

Cool the cake completely in the pan, then remove pan sides and transfer the cake on its base to a platter. Sift confectioners' sugar over the top and cut into wedges to serve.

Sospiri little cakes filled with pastry cream

Biting into one of these cream-filled glazed pastries inevitably elicits a sigh, the meaning of *sospiri*. They might remind you of a whoopie pie, their two cake layers bonded by a creamy filling, but I knew these well before I was introduced to the American dessert. In my hometown we referred to these as "*i dulci*"—our sweets. In fact, I grew up believing that they were a specialty of our town; it wasn't until later that I discovered their name, and that they were made and sold throughout Southern Italy.

My uncle Luigi learned to make the dessert from relatives in Serino, near Avellino. He was the sole person in Verbicaro who knew how to make them, and he guarded his secret recipe, allowing nobody to enter his house when he baked. People in town would put in special orders with him when they needed *sospiri* for an event. He stopped his craft only when a *pasticceria* opened in town, and people began to buy them there. Even now, nobody would give up a recipe; I was on my own to re-create it. When my mom pronounced mine better than the ones sold in the *pasticceria* back home, I knew they were ready to include here.

To produce the lightest cakes, have your eggs at room temperature before you begin—leave them on the counter overnight or put them into a bowl of warm water for 10 to 15 minutes. Make the *sospiri* a day or two in advance; they improve as the cake soaks up the filling and glaze.

CAKE

4 large eggs, separated, at room temperature

1/2 cup (100 g) granulated sugar

Finely grated zest from 1 small lemon

Pinch of kosher salt

2/3 cup (88 g) cake flour

GLAZE

2 cups (250 g) confectioners' sugar

2 tablespoons corn syrup or glucose syrup

3 tablespoons hot water

1/4 teaspoon pure vanilla extract

Chocolate or rainbow diavoletti (sprinkles) or candied cherries, for decoration (optional)

1 3/4 cups (480 g) pastry cream (page 185), cooled

To make the cake, beat the egg yolks, 1/4 cup of the sugar, and the lemon zest at high speed in a stand mixer with the whisk attachment, or with a handheld electric mixer, until pale yellow and thick, about 5 minutes.

In a clean bowl using clean beaters, beat the egg whites with a pinch of salt, beginning at medium-low speed until the whites are frothy, then increasing to medium speed until they are very thick and frothy. Slowly add the remaining 1/4 cup of sugar, a few teaspoons at a time, then beat at medium-high speed until the whites form firm, but not dry, peaks that hold their shape when the beater is lifted.

Use a large spatula to gently fold the egg yolks into the whites until mostly combined but still a little streaky. Sift the cake flour over the batter in six additions, gently folding in each addition, until the flour is completely and evenly incorporated, taking care not to deflate the batter.

Preheat the oven to 350°F (177°C) with racks in the upper and lower thirds of the oven. Line two baking sheets with parchment paper or silicone baking mats.

CONTINUED

Scoop the batter into a piping bag fitted with a $^5/_8$-inch round tip (Ateco #808). Pipe out 2-inch rounds with one inch all around them, forming sixteen rounds on each sheet. Bake just until the tops begin to lightly color, about 12 minutes, rotating the pans top to bottom and front to back halfway through baking.

Let the cakes cool completely on the baking sheets. When they are cool, slide a small offset spatula under the cakes to loosen them, turning them bottom side up and arranging them in matching pairs.

To make the glaze, whisk together the confectioners' sugar, corn syrup, hot water, and vanilla in a heatproof bowl. Place the bowl over a small pan of simmering water so that the bowl is over, but not touching, the water. Stir the glaze just until it is smooth and warm, about 1 minute. Remove the bowl from the pan and set it aside to cool slightly while you fill the *sospiri.*

To fill the cookies, spoon a heaping tablespoon of pastry cream evenly over half of the rounds, then sandwich them with their matching tops. Use a small offset spatula to smooth the pastry cream around the edges. Place the filled *sospiri* on a wire rack set over a rimmed baking sheet to catch the glaze.

Check the glaze: if it is cool and stiff, warm it over the simmering water, stirring, until it is thick and pourable. Pour the glaze over the *sospiri*, centering it over the tops so that it spreads to cover them and drips down over the edges. To decorate them as they do in Italian pastry shops, sprinkle the *sospiri* with *diavoletti* or place a candied cherry on top.

Let the glaze stand until dry to the touch, about 1 hour. Place each *sospiri* into a paper cupcake liner, then pack them in a single layer in an airtight container. Cover and refrigerate for 24 to 48 hours, or up to 4 days, before serving cold in their liners.

Pesche con Crema di Ricotta peach-shaped cakes filled with ricotta cream

After moving to California from Calabria, my mother and I insisted on crafting a recipe for these lovely little cakes so that we could enjoy them between trips back to Italy, where they are found in pastry shops and are not made at home. I included the recipe in my first cookbook, filling the peaches with plain pastry cream as those were the ones I knew. Since that time, traveling throughout Southern Italy, I've found them filled with ricotta cream, coffee pastry cream, chocolate, or even Nutella. The most fun part is fooling guests into thinking they are looking at a platter of small peaches—especially convincing when they are garnished with real peach tree leaves—then seeing their delight as they pick one up and discover it is a pastry.

Calabrian pastry chefs paint on Alchermes liqueur to blush their faux peaches. In the United States, I tint light rum with food coloring. Making the peaches a day or two ahead allows the alcohol to seep into the cakes, flavoring and softening them.

CAKES

4 cups (528 g) all-purpose flour

1 tablespoon baking powder

3 large eggs

3/4 cup (150 g) sugar

1/2 cup (120 ml) whole milk

1/2 cup (113 g) unsalted butter, melted and cooled

Finely grated zest of 1 lemon

2 cups (550 g) ricotta cream (page 188)

1/4 cup (60 ml) light rum

1/4 cup (60 ml) Italian maraschino liqueur (see Sources, page 203), or more rum

Red and yellow liquid or paste food coloring

1 cup (200 g) sugar, plus more as needed

A few peach tree leaves, or store-bought leaf decorations, for garnish (optional)

To make the cakes, preheat the oven to 350°F (177°C) with a rack in the center of the oven. Line two baking sheets with silicone baking mats or parchment paper.

Sift the flour and baking powder into a bowl. Whisk the eggs and sugar in a separate bowl with a fork. Whisk in the milk, butter, and lemon zest until smooth. Mix in the flour mixture in three or four additions, until everything is well incorporated, finishing the mixing with your hands. Press the dough into a ball and let it rest for 5 minutes.

Roll a slightly mounded tablespoon of dough between your palms to make a smooth, round ball. Continue to form balls of equal size, making a total of forty-eight of them, placing the balls on the baking sheets with about 1 inch space between them. When you have filled the first sheet of twenty-four balls, press down on the balls to slightly flatten them.

Bake until the cake bottoms are lightly browned (the tops will be pale), about 15 minutes, rotating the pan halfway through baking. Transfer the sheet to a wire rack just until the cakes are cool enough to handle. Form the second set as the first sheet bakes, and bake them after you have removed the first sheet from the oven.

While the cakes are still warm, use a paring knife to scoop out a teaspoon-size hollow from the flat side of each cake to hold the

CONTINUED

filling, taking care not to cut all the way through to the edges or top. (Save the cut out centers for filling Biscotti all'Amarena, page 72, or use them as cookie crumbs.)

Match up the cakes in similar-size pairs. Fill all of the cake hollows with a generous teaspoon of ricotta cream. Sandwich the flat sides of a filled cake pair together until the filling squeezes out just to the edge of the cakes. Gently run your finger around the seam to smooth and remove any excess cream.

To decorate the peaches, stir together the rum and maraschino liqueur in a small bowl. Add red and yellow food coloring, a drop or two at a time, until it turns a dark peach color, using a pastry brush to mix in the color. To test the color, brush a small amount on one of the filled cakes. If it is a bright pinkish-red (peach) color, you are ready.

Place 1 cup of sugar in a shallow bowl. Holding a filled cake over the peach-colored rum, dip the pastry brush in the rum and brush it over the cake on all sides, letting any excess drip back into the bowl. Set the cake on a wire rack for a minute to absorb a bit of the rum, then roll it in the sugar to give it an even coating of "peach fuzz." Continue until all of the peaches are colored and coated with sugar.

Carefully transfer the peaches to an airtight container lined with parchment paper. Refrigerate overnight before serving.

To serve, arrange the cakes on a footed fruit plate or cake stand to look like peaches. Garnish the cakes by inserting the stem of a peach leaf into a few of the peaches where the two cakes meet.

Tartufo ai Fichi Secchi con Miele di Fichi
ice cream "truffle" with dried figs and fig syrup

SERVES 8 | GLUTEN FREE

In *My Calabria*, I included a recipe for the famous *tartufo di Pizzo*, in which scoops of chocolate and hazelnut ice cream are filled with a liquid chocolate center. Here I am including another *tartufo*, this one representing the quintessential flavors of Calabria. I encountered this *tartufo* at Caffè Nìnì in Diamante, and the first bite brought back memories of the *crocette* my grandmother made by stuffing dried figs with walnuts. Caffè Nìnì makes more than twenty varieties of *tartufi*, including this one celebrating Calabria's much-loved Dottato (Kadota) figs.

For this *tartufo*, I've filled *fior di latte* (flower of milk) gelato with chopped figs and walnuts, then drizzled it with *miele di fichi*, a dark, honey-like syrup made from figs. More of the *miele di fichi* is ribboned through the ice cream.

Dried Kadota figs are difficult to find in America. Instead, look for the Calimyrna variety from California, or any Greek or Turkish white fig variety; they will appear darker once dried.

GELATO

1 cup (200 g) sugar

3 tablespoons cornstarch

3 cups (720 ml) whole milk

1 1/2 cups (360 ml) heavy cream

1/2 teaspoon pure vanilla extract

2 teaspoons miele di fichi, homemade (page 198) or store-bought (see Sources, page 203)

FILLING

4 to 5 (75 g) dried white figs, finely chopped

1/4 cup (28 g) finely chopped walnuts

1 tablespoon citron or orange marmalade, homemade (page 194) or store-bought

1 tablespoon miele di fichi, plus more for drizzling, homemade (page 198) or store-bought (see Sources, page 203)

To make the gelato, combine the sugar and cornstarch in a 2 1/2-quart saucepan. Whisk in the milk to completely dissolve the cornstarch. Stir in the cream. Bring the mixture to a boil over medium heat and continue to boil, stirring constantly, until it has the texture of a thick cream sauce, 8 to 10 minutes. Let cool, then refrigerate until very cold, about 4 hours. Stir in the vanilla.

Process the gelato in an ice cream maker according to the manufacturer's directions. Swirl in the *miele di fichi* as you pack the gelato into a container, using a spatula to draw it through the gelato in a ribbon. Cover and freeze until firm, at least 6 hours or overnight.

To make the filling, mix together the figs, walnuts, marmalade, and *miele di fichi* in a small bowl. Spoon out the filling into eight equal portions, using about 1 tablespoon for each.

To assemble the *tartufi*, line eight custard cups or 8-ounce ramekins with plastic wrap, pressing it against the cups and letting it drape over the edges on all sides. Use a scoop or measuring cup to scoop 1/2 cup of gelato into each cup. (If the ice cream is too firm to scoop, let it stand a few minutes to soften. If it becomes too soft, return it to the freezer for 15 to 30 minutes before continuing.)

CONTINUED

Use the back of a spoon to form a well in the center of each scoop, then fill the wells with the fig-walnut filling. Cover the filling with 1 tablespoon of gelato each, smoothing the gelato over the tops to enclose the filling. Fold the overhanging plastic wrap to cover the tops and freeze until firm, at least 2 hours or up to 1 week. (If frozen longer than a few hours, let the *tartufi* stand at room temperature for 15 minutes to soften before serving.)

To serve, unmold each *tartufo* by inverting it onto a plate or shallow bowl and removing the plastic wrap. Drizzle the tops with additional fig syrup, and serve immediately.

Gelato al Miele di Fichi fig ice cream topped with fig syrup

SERVES 8 TO 10 | GLUTEN FREE

This gelato comes from Pietro Lecce, chef of the renowned restaurant La Tavernetta in Camigliatello, located in the La Sila Mountains. I invited the chef to share a recipe for this book and asked if he might have something using figs. He grinned widely as he replied, "Wait until you taste my ice cream served with *miele di fichi*."

I was concerned that readers might have trouble finding sufficient fresh figs to make the *miele di fichi* (fig syrup) the way I always had, but he put those concerns to rest when he told me he'd come up with a way to make it using dried figs. I was delighted to learn I preferred the intense flavor of the *miele* made with his method to my own. The chef created this ice cream as a way to use the cooked figs left from making his *miele di fichi,* and he cleverly uses the *miele* as a sauce, along with a few almonds for crunch. Simple and superb.

2 cups (480 ml) whole milk

2 cups (480 ml) half-and-half

$^3/_4$ to 1 cup packed (200 to 250 g) cooked figs, left from making miele di fichi (page 198)

$^3/_4$ cup plus 2 tablespoons (175 g) sugar

Toasted sliced almonds, for topping

Miele di fichi, for drizzling, homemade (page 198) or store-bought (see Sources, page 203)

Bring the milk and half-and-half to a boil in a saucepan over medium heat. Remove from the heat and stir in the figs and sugar. Purée the mixture with an immersion blender until smooth. (Alternatively, carefully transfer the hot mixture to a blender and process until smooth.)

Transfer the mixture to a bowl and set it over a larger bowl of ice and water until cool, stirring occasionally, taking care not to slosh water into the mixture. Refrigerate until cold, at least 2 or up to 8 hours.

Process the mixture in an ice cream maker according to the manufacturer's directions. When it is ready, pack the gelato into an airtight container and freeze until firm, at least 4 hours or up to 1 week.

To serve, place two scoops of gelato in each bowl. Sprinkle with almonds and drizzle *miele di fichi* over the top.

Semifreddo di Liquirizia licorice frozen dessert

SERVES 12 | GLUTEN FREE

Pure licorice has little in common with the twisted red and black licorice-flavored sticks sold as candy. I remember sucking on wild licorice root as a child and loving its distinctive flavor. Extracted from the tough, gnarly roots of the licorice plant and prized the world over, Calabrian licorice is packaged in tins as *liquirizia spezzata,* small, intensely flavored, naturally sweet candies, with no sugar or any other ingredients added (see Sources, page 203). *Semifreddo* means half cold and is typically an ice cream terrine with a light, mousse-like texture. This one is made by folding beaten egg whites and whipped cream into an ice cream base.

1¹/₂ tablespoons pure licorice pieces, such as Amarelli spezzata

1 cup (240 ml) whole milk

4 large eggs, separated

³/₄ cup (150 g) sugar

Pinch of kosher salt

1¹/₄ cups (300 ml) heavy cream

Licorice liqueur, for drizzling (optional)

Put the licorice in a ziplock bag and pound it with a mallet or rolling pin to crush it into small pieces. Warm the milk in a 1¹/₂-quart saucepan over medium-low heat until it is steaming but not simmering. Add the licorice and stir until it dissolves completely. Remove from the heat.

Beat the egg yolks with ¹/₂ cup of the sugar in a stand mixer at high speed using the whisk attachment, until thick and pale, about 5 minutes. With the mixer on low to avoid scrambling the yolks, add the licorice-milk mixture in a slow stream. (Alternatively, use a handheld electric mixer.)

Return the mixture to the saucepan and cook over medium heat, stirring constantly with a wooden spoon, until the mixture thickens enough to coat the back of a spoon; do not boil. Transfer the mixture to a bowl set over a larger bowl filled with ice and water. Let cool, stirring occasionally and taking care not to slosh water into the mixture.

Beat the egg whites with a pinch of salt at high speed in a clean bowl using clean beaters until soft peaks form. Add the remaining ¹/₄ cup of sugar and continue beating until firm peaks form that are not at all dry.

In another bowl, whip the cream using an electric mixer until firm peaks form. Use a large spatula to gently fold the whites into the thickened milk mixture in three additions. Fold in the whipped cream until no streaks remain.

Line a 9- by 5-inch loaf pan with plastic wrap so that it overhangs the pan on all sides. Transfer the *semifreddo* mixture to the pan and level the top. Smooth the overhanging plastic wrap against the surface and freeze until firm, 6 to 8 hours.

To serve, remove the plastic wrap from the top and invert onto a serving platter. Peel away the plastic wrap and cut the *semifreddo* into ²/₃-inch-thick slices. Serve plain or with a drizzle of licorice liqueur.

Fichi Secchi al Cioccolato chocolate-dipped dried figs filled with almonds and candied orange peel

MAKES 24 CANDIES | GLUTEN FREE

In the late summer, when the golden figs on her trees were plump and sweet, my grandmother would begin the process of drying them. She would lay the figs outdoors on homemade reed trays, turning them every few days until they were dry enough to store for winter. In those days, Calabrians had no packaged candies, so people would devise their own sweets using the dried figs and the harvest from their nut trees, cutting a slit in the figs and stuffing them with almonds or walnuts, then drying them in a wood-burning oven so that they would last through the winter. My grandmother stuffed hundreds of pounds of figs every year, and my mother recalls taking a handful with her to the farm for a high-energy snack as she worked. As I was growing up, these chewy figs filled with crunchy nuts were our most common sweet, and my own children prefer them to the sugary candies available in the United States today.

Nowadays, Calabrian shops sell beautifully packaged and costly versions of the humble dried fig confections from rural Calabria. Modern confectioners make stuffed dried figs just as my grandmother did, often preserving them in rum syrup or dressing them up in a coat of dark chocolate.

I have made these chocolate-dipped figs for my family and friends for years without ever tempering the chocolate; we never minded that the coating wasn't perfectly shiny, nor that it would occasionally "bloom," with harmless white spots and streaks of cocoa butter rising to the surface. However, as I give bags of these figs as holiday gifts, I now temper the chocolate for a reliably smooth, glossy finish, prettier than anything I have seen in stores. If you aren't concerned about the figs looking perfect, simply melt the chocolate and dip the figs.

"Seeding" the chocolate by separating out and melting two-thirds of the chocolate, then stirring in the remainder in large chunks, is one of the easiest ways to temper it. You won't need all of the chocolate for this recipe, but you will have a much easier time tempering and dipping with this larger quantity. To save the remaining chocolate for baking or eating, scrape it out onto a piece of parchment paper, allow it to cool and harden, then wrap and store in the pantry.

24 dried Calimyrna or Kalamata figs

24 skin-on almonds

24 half-inch pieces (60 g) candied orange peel (page 193)

1 1/2 pounds (680 g) dark chocolate (65 to 70 percent cacao)

Preheat the oven to 275°F (135°C).

Gently flatten the figs with your fingers, pinching the sides together if the stems are buried in the center so that the stems are all at one end. Remove and discard the stems. Use a paring knife to cut a slit in the end of the fig opposite the stem, about 3/4 inch wide by 3/4 inch deep, pressing on the sides of the fig to open up a little pocket.

Press together an almond and a piece of orange peel and stuff them into the pocket, pinching the fig closed to hide the filling. Gently press the fig to flatten it and seal the opening.

CONTINUED

Bake the figs on an ungreased baking sheet for 40 minutes, turning them over halfway through. The figs will puff and darken slightly. When they are cool enough to handle, transfer the figs to a wire rack to cool completely.

Finely chop 1 pound of the chocolate. Cut the remaining ¹/₂ pound into three large chunks.

Holding back the large chunks, melt the chopped chocolate in a double boiler or in a bowl placed over, but not touching, about 1 inch of simmering water until the chocolate is smooth and the temperature registers 115° to 120°F (46° to 49°C).

Transfer the top of the double boiler to the counter, leaving the bottom over low heat to keep the water warm. Add the large chunks of chocolate to the melted chocolate, stirring until the temperature drops to 84°F (29°C), scraping down the sides of the bowl occasionally.

When the chocolate has reached 84°F (29°C), use a fork to remove any chunks of chocolate. Take the pan of warm water from the heat and set the top of the double boiler back over it. Stir continuously until the temperature climbs to 88°F (31°C), then remove the top from the double boiler, leaving the thermometer in place and watching it closely. Take care not to let the chocolate go over 90°F (32°C), which requires starting the tempering process over again.

Line a baking sheet with parchment paper. Working quickly to keep the chocolate from cooling (stir it over the warm water if the temperature falls too low), drop a fig into the chocolate and use a fork to submerge it completely. Retrieve the fig, scraping the fork against the edge of the bowl to remove any excess chocolate, then place the fig on the prepared pan.

After all of the figs have been dipped, set the baking sheet aside to allow the figs to cool and harden, about 2 hours. Stored in an airtight container with parchment paper separating the layers, the figs will keep for at least 6 months.

4

Puglia and Basilicata

Puglia and Basilicata share many of the same desserts, the majority of which originated in Puglia and spread to its pastoral neighbor. With the exception of the baroque city of Lecce (Puglia), this was never an area of great wealth or aristocratic importance. The desserts of these two regions, much like those of my Calabrian home, originated in local farmhouses rather than with celebrated pastry chefs. Instead of elaborate sweets, here are found wonderfully simple desserts developed by peasants using limited supplies and ample creativity.

Puglia is Italy's heel, its long coastline lapped on two sides by the Adriatic and Ionian seas. It is an area of beaches and grottoes and fields of flat agricultural land on which grow olive and (to a lesser extent) almond trees, grapevines, grains, fruits, and vegetables. (Puglia is Italy's largest producer of olive oil.) The area was colonized by the Greeks and was the endpoint of the Roman Via Appia, one of the earliest and most strategically important roads, connecting Rome at one end to Brindisi at the other. With the port towns of Brindisi and Bari once considered

the area's gateway to the East, the region is a melting pot of Eastern and Western cultures, showcasing the ornate Saracen influence alongside Roman-style architecture. Baroque-era buildings in the city of Lecce, often referred to as the Athens of Puglia, rival the most ornate in Sicily. This melting pot is played out in the area's simple sweets based on the local wheat, grapes, olive oil, honey, and ricotta combined with almonds and figs from the Adriatic Coast.

Neighboring Basilicata is nestled between Campania, Puglia, and Calabria, and its desserts are an amalgam of those areas. Rich in archaeological sites but otherwise historically poor, this isolated area has given birth to some of Southern Italy's best cooking, made from simple, rustic ingredients. The ancient town of Matera is one of the world's oldest continuously inhabited cities. Its rocky to mountainous, treeless landscape is the opposite of the lush woods found in Basilicata's north; its impoverished, barren cave dwellings are now being preserved and brought up to modern living standards as a UNESCO World Heritage Site.

In Basilicata, desserts are based on almonds, walnuts, figs, ricotta, citrus, and honey, as well as chestnuts at higher elevations. As elsewhere, sweets in Puglia and Basilicata have, for the most part, been reserved for holidays and special occasions.

Although many of the two region's desserts originated in the surrounding areas, some cookies remain largely unknown outside Puglia and Basilicata. In the town of Ceglie Messapica (Puglia) I found my favorite cookie, the *Biscotti di Ceglie* (page 162), made from the area's abundant almonds, ground and mixed with honey and limoncello, enclosing a bit of jam made from the local cherries. In Matera, *strazzate* (page 152) are rustic "torn" almond cookies, simple and crunchy. Walnuts grow abundantly in Strecchina and take center stage in the local cookies called *Dolci di Noci* (page 151). Also in Puglia I found local favorites *Intorchiate* (page 158), *Castagnelle* (page 164), and the bite-sized *Pezzetti di Cannella* (page 156), with their refreshing cinnamon finish.

Before sugar was widely available, the sweeteners of choice were *mosto cotto* (see page 197)—known in Puglia as *vino cotto*—and *miele di fichi* (page 198)—known locally as *cotto di fichi*. Puglia bakers use their local almonds to make a variety of *pasticcini di mandorla* (almond paste cookies) similar to those found in Sicily. The nuts are also ground into *pasta di mandorla* (page 190) and formed into the shape of a lamb at Easter and a large fish for Christmas. The almond paste figures are filled with *faldacchiera,* a mixture of cream and pear preserves and are still made today at the monastery of San Giovanni Evangelista in Lecce. Also found in Lecce is the *pasticciotto*, a small oval pastry made of *pasta frolla* (page 183), filled with pastry cream, the whole thing dusted with confectioners' sugar. The sweet is often eaten warm for breakfast. The little tarts called *bocconotti* (page 121) are found in both regions, with a variety of fillings, from pastry cream to ricotta, almond paste, and assorted jams.

As elsewhere, holidays herald a parade of sweets. In March, the feast of San Giuseppe, celebrated as Father's Day, brings fried or baked *zeppole* (similar to doughnuts) borrowed from neighboring Campania, here topped with pastry cream and *amarene,* the local preserved cherries. Carnevale is the time for *Chiacchiere* (page 117), strips of sweet dough fried and coated with confectioners' sugar. For Easter, the traditional sweet breads called *scarcelle* are shaped like dolls and baskets, decorated with a cross, an egg still in its shell baked into them. The sweetened bread would not be considered a dessert by American standards. Also popular here at Easter, but also found year-round in bakeries, are the wreath-shaped *taralli* cookies coated with a sugar glaze, and *Barchiglia* (page 170), a sweet pastry dough encasing a filling of pear preserves and almond paste, all covered with chocolate. As in other parts of Southern Italy, *grano cotto,* or cooked wheat, is eaten in both of these regions for All Souls' Day, here dressed up with *mosto cotto*, nuts, and pomegranate seeds.

Finishing out the year, a simple dessert of fried yeasted dough known as *pettole* or *pittule* begins showing up in the area of Taranto for the Feast of Saint Cecilia, on November 22, and continues through the Christmas holidays and up to the Epiphany, on January 6. At Christmas, *cartellate* (page 173), originally from Puglia but now also found in Basilicata (where they are known as *carteddate or crespelle*) were traditionally coated with *mosto cotto* (see page 197) or *miele di fichi* (see page 198). These days, when few people are keeping the tradition of making their own syrups, honey may be used in its place. Similar to the Neapolitan s*truffoli, purcidduzzi* are another favorite Christmas treat. Ravioli-shaped pillows called *Calzoncelli* (page 177) filled with a paste of sweetened chickpeas or chestnuts are a Christmas favorite in Basilicata and are also found in Calabria and Puglia.

Dolci di Noci walnut cookies

I found these crunchy-chewy cookies in the pastry shops of Maratea. When I asked if they were typical of the area, I was told that they originally came from Trecchina, the next town over. Indeed, these are the only two towns in Basilicata where they are found.

A simple mixture of just three ingredients, the cookies could hardly be easier to make. In pastry shops, the cookies will likely be topped with a thick white sugar *glassa* (glaze), sometimes with a red stripe made from the syrup of preserved amarena cherries, but I think this only masks their intense walnut flavor. If you wish to make them as they do in Trecchina, prepare the *glassa* (glaze) from Biscotti all'Amarena (page 72) and brush a swath of it over the cookie tops just after pulling them from the oven, adding the red line of cherry syrup described in that recipe if you wish. The heat of the cookie will set the glaze.

2^{1}/$_{2}$ cups (285 g) walnut
halves or large pieces

1 cup (200 g) sugar

1 large egg

Pictured on pages 154–155

Preheat the oven to 375°F (190°C) with a rack in the upper third of the oven. Line a baking sheet with parchment paper or a silicone baking mat.

Combine the walnuts and sugar in a food processor and process to make a fine meal the texture of sand. Transfer to a bowl. Make a well in the middle and add the egg. Use a fork to briefly whisk the egg, then begin incorporating the nuts until everything is thoroughly combined, finishing the mixing with your hands. The dough will be quite moist and a little sticky.

Divide the dough into quarters. On a flat surface, shape one piece of the dough into a 6-inch log, flattening the sides to make a bar about 1 inch wide by 1 inch high. Cut the bar into ^{3}/$_{4}$ inch segments to make eight pieces. Space the cookies evenly on the prepared baking sheet, standing on their base (not on a cut side) with 1 inch of space all around for spreading. Repeat with the remaining bars to make thirty-two cookies.

Bake the cookies on the upper oven rack until they are golden all over, about 15 minutes. Let cool on the pan. Store leftover cookies in an airtight container for up to 2 weeks.

Strazzate *"torn" almond cookies*

Strazzate is dialect for torn or ripped, which is how these rough-textured cookies look. Crunchy on the outside, moist on the inside, this traditional sweet used to be made at Christmastime in Matera but is now found in the town's bakeries all year round. People I spoke with mentioned replacing a tablespoon of the coffee with Strega liqueur, or adding a couple of ounces of chopped dark chocolate to the batter, as common variations. You can try that if you like, but I like them best the way I've made them here.

2 cups (264 g) all-purpose flour

1³/₄ cups (263 g) almonds, toasted and chopped medium-fine

1 cup (200 g) sugar

1 teaspoon baking powder

¹/₄ teaspoon kosher salt

Finely grated zest of 1 lemon

1 large egg

¹/₄ cup (60 ml) extra-virgin olive oil

¹/₄ cup (60 ml) prepared espresso or strong coffee

Pictured on pages 154–155

Preheat the oven to 400°F (204°C) with a rack in the upper third of the oven. Line two baking sheets with parchment paper or silicone baking mats.

In a bowl, stir together the flour, almonds, sugar, baking powder, salt, and lemon zest. Make a well in the center and add the egg, oil, and coffee. Use a fork to whisk the wet ingredients together, then incorporate the dry ingredients. When the dough becomes difficult to mix, use your hands to mix until everything is well incorporated. The dough will be stiff and slightly sticky.

Pinch off 2 level tablespoons of dough and place on one of the prepared baking sheets. Leave the cookies looking like uneven jumbles—they should look "torn," not rolled into smooth balls. Continue to pinch off similar-size pieces of dough to make sixteen cookies.

Bake on the upper oven rack until the cookies are golden and feel dry to the touch, about 15 minutes, rotating the pan front to back halfway through baking. Transfer the cookies to a wire rack to cool.

While the first sheet bakes, form the remaining cookies on the second sheet. Bake the second sheet after pulling the first from the oven.

Store the cooled cookies in an airtight container at room temperature for up to 2 weeks. They will continue to dry and get crunchier over time.

Quaresimali chunky almond biscotti

MAKES 24 COOKIES

The *quaresimali* found in much of Southern Italy are similar to the *cantucci* of Northern Italy—what we think of in the United States as biscotti. I found this chewy-centered version at Caffè Tripoli in Martina Franca (Puglia). Loaded with chopped toasted almonds, they are my new favorite cookie.

Traditionally made for Quaresima, or Lent, when no fat was to be used in cooking, these cookies lack the egg yolks found in other biscotti. However, the rich sheen on the ones I found in Puglia looked suspiciously as if they had been glazed with an egg yolk wash, which makes sense because the cookies contain egg whites.

The second baking (the "bis" in biscotti) is not imperative. Baked only once, they have an appealing chewy texture. Even better, though, is the contrast of chew and crunch that comes from crisping the outside with a second baking.

2 cups (300 g) almonds, toasted lightly

1 cup (200 g) sugar

1/2 cup (66 g) all-purpose flour

2 tablespoons packed minced candied orange peel (page 193)

Finely grated zest of one orange

1/4 teaspoon ground cinnamon

1 large egg, separated

1 large egg white

1/2 teaspoon pure vanilla extract

1 teaspoon water

Pictured on pages 154–155

Preheat the oven to 350°F (177°C) with a rack in the center. Line a baking sheet with parchment paper or a silicone baking mat.

Pulse the almonds in a food processor until they are chopped to a medium size. Tap the work bowl on the counter to bring the largest pieces to the top, pull those out, and chop them by hand to a medium-fine texture. (Continuing to process the nuts will make the smaller pieces too fine.) Transfer all of the chopped almonds to a bowl and add the sugar, flour, candied orange peel, zest, and cinnamon. Stir with a fork to combine.

Use a fork to whisk the 2 egg whites with the vanilla in a small bowl until foamy. Make a well in the middle of the almond mixture and add the whites. Mix well, starting with a fork and continuing with your hands to form a sticky dough that holds together when you press it. Divide the dough in two and place one piece along one long side of the prepared pan. Shape the dough into an 11-inch by 2 1/2-inch loaf that is about 3/4 inch high. Make a second loaf with the remaining dough parallel to the first one.

Whisk the egg yolk with the water in a small bowl. Brush the egg wash over the tops of the dough.

Bake until golden brown all over, about 25 minutes, rotating the pan front to back halfway through baking. Let the loaves cool on the sheet until you can easily handle them, about 15 minutes. Leave the oven on.

Trim the ends from the loaves (enjoy as a snack) and cut each loaf into twelve slices about 3/4 inch wide. Return the slices to the baking sheet, cut side down, and bake for 5 to 10 minutes to dry them.

Store the cookies in an airtight container for up to 1 week.

CLOCKWISE FROM TOP LEFT:
Pezzetti di Cannella (page 156),
Intorchiate (page 158), Biscotti di Ceglie (page 162),
Dolci di Noci (page 151), Castagnelle (page 164),
Strazzate (page 152), Quaresimali (page 153)

Pezzetti di Cannella little cinnamon cookies

MAKES 120 BITE-SIZE COOKIES

My mother's friend Yolanda Tateo shared her mother's recipe for these cookies. Yolanda moved to the United States from Sava (Puglia) when she was in her twenties. This is one of the few recipes from home that she has kept over the years.

These bite-sized cookies are perfect to have on hand for visitors or to enjoy with a cup of coffee or tea. It's worth splurging on good-quality cinnamon because it is the predominant flavoring. The recipe makes a lot of cookies; they can be stored for up to a month in an airtight container.

2 cups (264 g) all-purpose flour, plus more for rolling

$^1/_2$ cup (100 g) granulated sugar

2 tablespoons unsweetened Dutch-processed cocoa powder

1 tablespoon ground cinnamon

2 teaspoons baking powder

2 large eggs

$^1/_4$ cup (60 ml) safflower or other neutral-tasting vegetable oil

2 tablespoons whole milk

Finely grated zest of 1 lemon

GLAZE

2 cups (250 g) confectioners' sugar, plus more as needed

5 tablespoons (75 ml) fresh lemon juice

Pictured on pages 154–155

Preheat the oven to 350°F (177°C) with racks in the upper and lower thirds of the oven. Line two baking sheets with parchment paper or silicone baking mats.

Sift the flour, sugar, cocoa, cinnamon, and baking powder into a large bowl. Make a well in the center and add the eggs, oil, milk, and lemon zest. Mix the wet ingredients into the flour mixture with a fork until the flour is mostly incorporated, then continue by kneading with your hands in the bowl until the dough comes together into a smooth ball. Cover and set aside for 30 minutes.

Divide the dough into four pieces. Take one piece and, using a bit of flour if needed, roll it with your hands on a flat surface to form a rope about $^5/_8$ inch wide. Press down to slightly flatten the rope, then cut it on the diagonal into 1-inch diamond-shaped pieces. Arrange the cookies on the prepared baking sheets with an inch between them. Repeat to form cookies with the remaining three pieces of dough. (I form half of the cookies, then bake them while I form the second half.)

Bake until the cookies are puffed and firm to the touch, 10 to 12 minutes. Transfer the pans to wire racks until the cookies are completely cool, at least 1 hour.

To glaze the cookies, in a wide, shallow bowl large enough to hold all the cookies, use a whisk to stir the confectioners' sugar and lemon juice together to form a thick, smooth glaze. If the glaze is too thin, add a bit more sugar. Line two baking sheets with parchment paper. Put all of the cookies into the glaze at once and use your hands to coat them on all sides. Transfer the cookies one at a time to the prepared baking sheets—the glaze should cling to the cookies without pooling on the sheet. Let the cookies stand until the glaze is completely dry, which can take up to 24 hours, before packing them into an airtight container.

Intorchiate almond cookie twists

Intorchiate is local dialect for intertwined, and this simple cookie from Puglia is meant to represent arms held in an embrace. Traditionally made for baptisms and marriages, the cookie symbolizes the union between the baby and God, or between spouses. Today, however, they are found in bakeries all over Puglia and are enjoyed with a cup of coffee or as an everyday snack.

3³/₄ cups (500 g) all-purpose flour

³/₄ cup (150 g) granulated sugar, plus more for coating cookies

1 tablespoon baking powder

¹/₄ teaspoon kosher salt

¹/₄ cup (56 g) unsalted butter, softened

¹/₄ cup (60 ml) extra-virgin olive oil

³/₄ cup (180 ml) white wine

About ³/₄ cup (115 grams) blanched almonds (page 189), for decorating

Pictured on pages 154–155

Combine the flour, sugar, baking powder, and salt in a food processor and pulse to combine. Add the butter, oil, and wine and process until the mixture forms a sticky dough that balls up around the blade. (Alternatively, you can mix the dough by hand, but it will require longer kneading to bring the dough together.) Transfer to a flat surface and knead briefly to form a smooth dough. Wrap the dough in plastic wrap and refrigerate for at least 1 hour, or up to 4 hours.

Preheat the oven to 350°F (177°C) with racks in the upper and lower thirds of the oven. Line two baking sheets with parchment paper or silicone baking mats.

Divide the dough into thirty-six approximately equal pieces; they will weigh about ³/₄ ounce each. Roll a piece of dough with the palms of your hands against a flat surface to make a 10-inch rope that is about ¹/₂ inch thick. Fold the rope in half, then twist the two ends around one another to form a twist, with the dough strands crossing twice and meeting at the bottom to form three spaces. Press the ends together at the bottom to seal them. Space the cookies 1 inch apart on the prepared baking sheet. Continue forming the twists until you have filled one

sheet with eighteen cookies. (You will make the second half while the first ones bake.)

Put about $1/4$ cup sugar in a shallow bowl. Take one cookie at a time and press the top side into the sugar. Return the cookie to the baking sheet sugar side up. After coating all of the cookies, press three blanched almonds into each cookie—one in each space—facing the pointed ends of the nuts running down from the top to the bottom of the cookie.

Bake the cookies on the bottom rack for 15 minutes, then rotate the pan and transfer it to the top rack until the cookies are light golden all over, about 15 minutes longer. Transfer the cookies to a wire rack to cool.

While the first sheet bakes, form the remaining cookies on the second sheet. Bake the second sheet in the same manner after pulling the first from the oven.

Store the cooled cookies in an airtight container at room temperature for up to 2 weeks.

Biscotti di Ceglie almond cookies with cherry preserves

MAKES ABOUT 36 SMALL COOKIES | GLUTEN FREE

These chunky almond cookies filled with preserves are a specialty of the town of Ceglie Messapica, one of the oldest towns in Puglia, located in the northern Salento area. They have been recognized by the Presidio of Slow Food as a unique specialty of this area made with local artisanal products. I'd read about the cookies but had never seen a recipe, so I set about creating my own. Later, I scouted them out on a trip to Puglia, where, after visiting a couple of pastry shops, I found that my version was every bit as good as theirs. I also found several variations, even within the town of Ceglie Messapica itself—some identical to mine, some with finer almonds, others using coffee rather than the typical limoncello, which nearly every Southern Italian family makes and keeps on hand. (Moistening your hands with the limoncello keeps the sticky dough manageable and also adds a lovely flavor.) I was cautioned that the cookies would not be as good without the local almonds, but California almonds provided excellent results.

4 cups (600g) blanched almonds (page 189), toasted and cooled

³/₄ cup (150 g) sugar

2 large eggs

2 tablespoons limoncello, homemade (page 200) or store-bought, plus more for forming the cookies

1 tablespoon mild-flavored honey, such as clover or orange blossom

Finely grated zest of 1 lemon

6 tablespoons (90 ml) cherry preserves

Pictured on pages 154–155

Combine the almonds and sugar in a food processor and process until they are coarsely ground, with pieces ranging in size from finely chopped almonds to coarse meal; they should have some texture. Transfer the nuts to a bowl and mix in the eggs, limoncello, honey, and lemon zest until well combined, finishing the mixing with your hands, if needed, to make a sticky ball of dough. Let rest uncovered for 30 minutes.

Preheat the oven to 375°F (190°C) with a rack in the upper third of the oven. Line a baking sheet with parchment paper or a silicone baking mat.

Use your hands to moisten a flat surface with limoncello. Transfer the dough to the moistened surface and cut it into thirds. Moisten your hands with a bit of limoncello to keep the dough from sticking. Flatten one piece of dough into a 4¹/₂-inch by 6¹/₂-inch rectangle. With a long side of the dough facing you, use 2 tablespoons of cherry preserves to form a ribbon along the lower third of the dough, running parallel to a long side about 1¹/₂ inches from the edge. Use a bench scraper or spatula to lift the front end of the dough up and over the filling to completely enclose it, pressing and rolling to seal the seam. Continue rolling the log gently under your (limoncello-moistened) hands to lengthen it to 13 inches long. Set the log seam side down and press down gently until it is about 1¹/₄ inches high. Use a sharp knife or bench scraper to cut it into 1-inch segments. Evenly space

the cookies about 1 inch apart on the prepared baking sheet as you form them, bottom side down, using the bench scraper to transfer the sticky cookies to the baking sheet. Repeat twice more to form cookies from the remaining dough.

Bake until the cookies are deep golden brown, 18 to 20 minutes. Transfer the baking sheet to a wire rack to cool. When they are cool enough to handle, transfer the cookies directly to the racks to cool completely. Store leftover cookies in an airtight container at room temperature for up to 2 weeks.

Castagnelle crunchy cinnamon-almond cookies

The Italian word for chestnut is *castagna,* and indeed, these Pugliese cookies resemble little chestnuts, though they contain none. These rustic cookies have none of the usual rich ingredients: not eggs, nor butter, nor even milk. In fact, the simplest version is made with water, though coffee adds flavor and the characteristic chestnut color.

These cookies go by *castagnedde* in the local Pugliese dialect. A similar cookie found in Basilicata is known as *pizzicannelli,* or little pieces of cinnamon, which are sometimes covered with a chocolate glaze.

2 cups (264 g) all-purpose flour

1¹/₃ cups (267 g) granulated sugar

1²/₃ cup (250 g) almonds, toasted and coarsely chopped

2 tablespoons unsweetened Dutch-processed cocoa powder

2 teaspoons baking powder

1 teaspoon ground cinnamon

Finely grated zest of 1 lemon

¹/₂ cup plus 2 tablespoons (150 ml) brewed espresso, strong coffee, or water

Confectioners' sugar, for finishing

Pictured on pages 154–155

Preheat the oven to 350°F (177°C) with racks in the upper and lower thirds of the oven. Line two baking sheets with parchment paper or silicone baking mats.

Stir together the flour, granulated sugar, almonds, cocoa, baking powder, cinnamon, and lemon zest in a large bowl. Make a well in the center and add the espresso, then mix into the dry ingredients until it is evenly incorporated. Continue to knead the dough with your hands in the bowl to make a stiff dough the texture of modeling clay. Divide the dough into quarters.

Using a bit of flour, if needed, roll a piece of dough into a rope about 20 inches long and 1 inch wide. Press down to slightly flatten the rope, then use a sharp knife or bench scraper to cut the rope on the diagonal into 1¹/₄ inch diamonds. As you make them, arrange the cookies on the prepared baking sheets, leaving at least ¹/₂ inch between them. Repeat with the remaining dough.

Bake until the cookies feel set but are still somewhat soft, about 15 minutes. The tops will crack but the cookies will not darken any further. Transfer the baking sheets to wire racks to cool. When they are cool enough to handle, transfer the cookies directly to the racks to cool completely. Sift confectioners' sugar generously over the cookies. Store the cookies in an airtight container for up to 2 weeks.

Grano dei Morti cooked wheat topped with chocolate, nuts, and pomegranate seeds

SERVES 8

Grano dei morti, or wheat of the dead, has been made to celebrate the Day of the Dead in the area around Foggia and Bari since the time the Greeks settled there. In Puglia the dessert is also known as *cicci cotti,* and in the Salento area as *colva.* The ancient Greeks used the wheat and pomegranate seeds as an offering to Demeter, goddess of the harvest, and her daughter Persephone. As the story goes, when Persephone was abducted into the underworld of Hades, she tasted the seeds of the pomegranate.

Pomegranates grow all over Italy, as well as in my California garden, so I seed them myself. To save you the trouble, many markets sell the seeds in small tubs in the produce section. Many families also add candied citron. If you can find imported Italian candied citron, often labeled *cedro candito,* add the diced pieces if you like, but please avoid the plastic supermarket tubs of candied citron meant for making fruit cakes. Hard and unpleasant, they taste nothing of the large, fragrant, pebbly-rind fruit so highly prized in my native country. If you can find fresh citron, you can make your own candied citron with its thick peel—which comprises most of the fruit—following the instructions for Scorze d'Arance Candite (candied orange peel) on page 193.

Once you've cooked the wheat, the remaining ingredient quantities should be guided entirely by your taste: there is no strict formula, so long as you get a little crunch and burst of flavor in every bite.

1 cup (200 g) wheat berries

6 cups (1.5 L) water, plus more for soaking the wheat berries

1 teaspoon kosher salt

²/₃ cup (105 g) pomegranate seeds (1 large pomegranate)

¹/₄ cup (28 g) walnuts, toasted and coarsely chopped

¹/₄ cup (37 g) almonds, toasted and coarsely chopped

Generous ¹/₃ cup (56 g) chopped dark chocolate (55 to 65 percent cacao) or chocolate chips

¹/₄ cup (60 ml) mosto cotto (page 197), plus more for drizzling

Ground cinnamon (optional)

Put the wheat berries in a bowl and cover with 4 cups of cold water. Cover and let stand at room temperature for 3 days, draining off and replacing the water once a day.

Drain the wheat berries and transfer them to a 4-quart saucepan. Add 6 cups of the water and the salt. Bring to a boil, then adjust the heat to cook the berries at a simmer, uncovered, until they are tender and most of them have split, about 90 minutes, adding water if needed to keep the wheat berries covered by about an inch.

Remove the pan from the heat and let the berries cool completely in the liquid. Drain and transfer the berries to a bowl.

Shortly before serving, stir in the pomegranate seeds, walnuts, almonds, and chocolate, adjusting the quantities as you wish. Stir in the *mosto cotto* and cinnamon, if you are using it, to taste. Spoon into individual bowls and serve at room temperature, drizzled with a bit more of the *mosto cotto,* if you like.

Crostata al Caprino sweet goat cheese tart

SERVES 8 TO 10

While visiting Matera (Basilicata), I was delighted to meet Francesco Abbondanza, owner of the restaurant Lucaniere, where I had been hoping to sample his highly reputed cuisine. Sadly, he had closed the restaurant while working on a new project, a store called L'Abbondanza Lucana. When I mentioned that I'd hoped to discover an innovative dessert or two at his restaurant, he began to describe his specialty—a tart filled with a rich mousse made with the local goat cheese, topped with seasonal fruits. He explained the process and urged me to try making it. I was delighted when I did.

Though I never had the chance to taste Abbondanza's tart, this one follows the process he shared with me. Simple and delicious, it is easily adapted to the seasons, crowned with berries in spring, sliced nectarines or peaches in summer, and fresh figs in fall. In winter, Abbondanza tops the tart with preserves he makes using the amarena cherries that grow abundantly in that area. As on a cheese plate, just about any fruit, fresh or preserved, seems to pair well with the sweet-tangy goat cheese filling. Choose a mild, creamy-style goat cheese, such as chèvre, or what the Italians refer to as *caprino* (*capra* is Italian for goat).

Short-crust pastry (page 183, single crust)

10 ounces (285 g) fresh goat cheese, at room temperature

2/3 cup (83 g) confectioners' sugar, plus more for finishing

Finely grated zest of 1 lemon

1 1/2 cups (360 ml) heavy cream

Fresh berries, other fruits, or preserves, for topping the tart

Make the pastry dough, flatten it into a disk, wrap in plastic wrap, and chill for at least 1 hour.

Butter a 9-inch tart pan with a removable bottom. Roll the pastry dough into a 12-inch round. Transfer the dough to the tart pan, settling it into the pan and pressing it against the bottom and sides. Trim the overhang flush with the edge. (The scraps can be rolled, cut, and baked as cookies.) Prick the bottom all over with a fork. Cover with plastic wrap and refrigerate for 30 minutes, or up to 1 hour.

Preheat the oven to 350°F (177°C) with a rack in the center of the oven. Butter a piece of parchment paper and place it buttered side down over the tart shell, then cover with dried beans or pie weights. Bake for 15 minutes, then remove the parchment paper and the weights and return the shell to the oven until it is golden around the sides and fully cooked on the bottom, 8 to 10 minutes longer. Let the shell cool completely in the pan.

Once the shell is cool, prepare the filling. Put the goat cheese in a bowl and use a spatula to smooth it. Mix in the confectioners' sugar and lemon zest until completely incorporated. Set aside.

Whip the cream with an electric mixer until firm peaks form. Use a large spatula to fold about one-quarter of the whipped cream into

CONTINUED

the goat cheese to lighten it, then fold in the remaining cream, gently bringing up the mixture from the bottom over the top to completely incorporate it without losing too much air.

Spread the mousse evenly into the tart shell, smoothing the top. Cover with plastic wrap and refrigerate until the mousse is set, 2 to 4 hours, or overnight.

To serve, remove the outer rim of the pan and place the tart on its base on a serving plate, or slide it off the base directly onto the plate if you wish. Completely cover the top of the tart with berries or other fruits in a decorative pattern. Sift confectioners' sugar over the top and cut into wedges.

Barchiglia chocolate-glazed almond tart with pear preserves

This dessert from Puglia is traditionally served for Pasqua (Easter), but it also may be found year round in the pastry shops of Lecce, made into individual pastries called *fruttone*. The small pastries are similar to *pasticciotto*, in which pastry cream is enclosed in *pasta frolla*. Barchiglia is traditionally made with a single crust, and I think the proportion of *pasta frolla* to filling is just right as I have it here. If you wish to add a top crust to enclose the pastry, use the two-crust short-crust recipe, rolling the second piece to use as the top crust, and pouring the glaze over the top after baking. (I like it equally well without the glaze.)

One of my favorite fruit preserves from this region, *marmellata di pere* is difficult to find outside Puglia. I've bumped up the amount used in the tart from what you would typically find in Puglia to allow it to shine through the chocolate and almond, but you'll be pleased to find that there's still plenty left to spread on your morning toast. Even if you don't make the tart, I urge you to make a batch of the *marmellata*.

Short-crust pastry (page 183, single crust)

1 cup (150 g) blanched almonds (page 189)

3 large eggs, separated

3/4 cup (150 g) sugar

1/4 teaspoon ground cinnamon

Finely grated zest of 1 lemon

Pinch of kosher salt

1 cup (330 g) Marmellata di Pere (recipe follows)

CHOCOLATE GLAZE

1/2 cup (120 ml) heavy cream

4 ounces (113 g) dark chocolate (60 to 65 percent cacao), coarsely chopped

Make the pastry dough, flatten it into a disk, wrap in plastic wrap, and chill for at least 1 hour,

Preheat the oven to 350°F (177°C) with a rack in the center of the oven. Butter a 9-inch tart pan with a removable bottom.

Roll the pastry dough into a 12-inch round. Transfer the dough to the tart pan, settling it into the pan and pressing it against the bottom and sides. Trim the overhang flush with the edge. Prick the bottom all over with a fork. Refrigerate until ready to fill.

To make the filling, process the almonds in a food processor until they have the texture of coarse meal. Set aside.

Beat the egg yolks and sugar at medium-high speed in a stand mixer with the whisk attachment until fluffy, about 2 minutes. (Alternatively, use a handheld mixer.) Use a spatula to mix in the cinnamon, lemon zest, and the reserved ground almonds until thoroughly incorporated. The mixture will be thick.

In a clean bowl with clean beaters, beat the egg whites with a pinch of salt at medium-high speed until they hold peaks that are firm but not at all dry. Use a large spatula to gently fold the egg whites into the almond mixture in three additions.

Remove the tart pan from the refrigerator and spread the pear preserves over the bottom in an even layer. Pour the almond filling over the preserves and use a spatula to level it. Bake until golden and puffed, about 40 minutes. A toothpick tested near the center should come out clean. Transfer the tart to a wire rack until it is completely cool (the tart will deflate a bit), then remove the outer ring of the tart pan and transfer the pan on its base to a serving plate.

To make the glaze, bring the cream to a simmer in a small saucepan. Turn off the heat and add the chopped chocolate. Let stand a few minutes to melt, then stir until smooth. Let the glaze cool until it is slightly thickened and spreadable, about 10 minutes.

Pour the chocolate glaze over the center of the tart, then use a spatula to nudge it outward to the edge of the filling, avoiding running it over the sides. Let the tart stand until the glaze is set before serving, about 2 hours.

Marmellata di Pere Pear preserves

MAKES A GENEROUS 3 CUPS | GLUTEN FREE

I use Bartlett pears for these preserves, but you can use whatever type you like. Choose pears that are ripe but still somewhat firm. Note that some types of pears will turn a lovely shade of rose as they cook.

3 pounds (1360 g) firm-ripe pears, peeled and cored

2³/₄ cups (550 g) sugar

Finely grated zest of 1 lemon

¹/₄ cup (60 ml) fresh lemon juice

Cut the pears into ¹/₂- to ³/₄-inch pieces and put them in a large saucepan. Stir in the sugar, lemon zest, and lemon juice. Let stand for 1 hour to draw out the pears' juice.

Bring the mixture to a boil over medium heat, then simmer slowly until the pears are translucent and the syrup is reduced and light golden, about 45 minutes. It should read about 215°F (102°C) on a candy thermometer. Let cool completely. Store in a glass jar in the refrigerator for up to 1 month.

Cartellate fried pastry rosettes bathed in mosto cotto

Cartellate or *carteddate* is the traditional Christmas dessert in Puglia and Basilicata, made by rolling dough until it is very thin and forming it into fluted rings with small pockets, then frying and coating them in *mosto cotto* or honey. I could find no consistent story about the name, but some believe the shape is meant to represent the halo around the baby Jesus or the swaddling cloth used to wrap him, while others contend that it mimics the crown of thorns placed atop his head at his crucifixion.

There are as many variations of the dough as there are families in Puglia, with some adding only wine and oil to the flour, others incorporating water or an egg, and some including a bit of sugar. One thing on which all in Puglia agree: The fried dough must be thin and crispy.

Traditionally, the fried sweets were bathed in warm *vino cotto* or *mosto cotto* (page 197) or with *cotto di fichi* (fig syrup, similar to *miele di fichi,* page 198). Nowadays, honey often takes their place, as many have abandoned making these syrups at home. Some people will sprinkle cinnamon or confectioners' sugar over the cookies, or top them with chopped toasted walnuts, almonds, or multicolor sprinkles. My preference: a simple coating of *mosto cotto*.

2 cups (264 g) all-purpose flour

1 tablespoon sugar

$^1/_3$ cup (80 ml) white wine

1 large egg

2 tablespoons olive oil, plus more for frying

$1^1/_2$ to 2 cups (360 to 480 ml) mosto cotto (page 197) or honey, for coating

Chopped toasted walnuts (optional)

Rainbow diavoletti (sprinkles) (optional)

Stir the flour and sugar with a fork in a bowl. Make a well in the center and add the wine, egg, and oil. Mix the wet ingredients with the fork, then begin incorporating the flour mixture until it is completely incorporated. Finish the mixing using your hands.

Transfer the dough to a flat surface and knead for several minutes to form a smooth, elastic dough that springs back when you poke it with your finger. Wrap the dough in plastic wrap and let it rest for 30 minutes.

To form the *cartellate,* line a baking sheet with a clean kitchen towel. Divide the dough into six pieces. Working with one piece at a time and leaving the others covered to avoid drying the dough, roll the dough with a pasta machine. Flatten the piece of dough and run it through the machine at the widest setting, then fold it in half and run it through again at the same setting. Continue to run the dough through the machine (without folding) twice at each setting until you reach the setting before last (#6 on my Atlas pasta machine). Roll the dough only once at the second-to-last setting. It should be about $^1/_{16}$ inch thick. Transfer the dough to a flat surface and trim it with a fluted cutter into a 12-inch by 4-inch rectangle. (Alternatively, use a rolling pin to roll the dough into a 12-inch by 4-inch rectangle about

CONTINUED

$^1/_{16}$ inch thick.) Cut the dough the long way with the fluted cutter into three strips, each $1^1/_4$ inches wide. (Collect and cover scraps as you go to make additional *cartellate*.)

Pick up one of the strips and, starting about an inch from one end, pull up the two sides as if you were folding the dough in half the long way and pinch them tightly together. Continue to pull up and tightly pinch the dough at about 1-inch intervals to form about six little pockets along the length of the dough, leaving the ends open. To form the rosette, starting at one end, pick up the dough and wrap it around to meet the strip between the first and second pockets; pinch to attach. This will form the center of the rosette. Now, working from the opposite end, bring the strip all the way around to encircle the first fold; pinch to attach, then continue to wrap and pinch to form a spiral, or rosette, taking care to leave the pockets open. Some leave the end open while others pinch it closed; either will work. Move the rosette to one end of the baking sheet. Continue to form the rosettes until you have used all of the dough, including the last piece made up of scraps. (If you need additional work space, lay a kitchen towel on a flat surface as a work area.) Let the rosettes dry, uncovered, for at least 2 hours, or up to 8 hours.

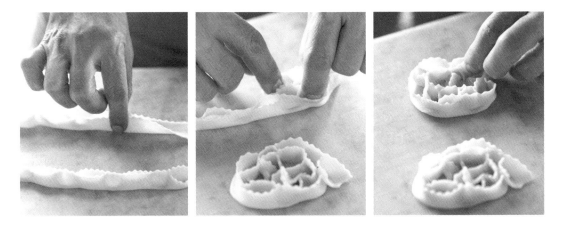

To fry the *cartellate*, have ready a baking sheet lined with paper towels. Heat 2 inches of oil in a large, wide (4- to 6-quart) saucepan over medium-high heat to 375°F (190℃). When it is ready, use a metal skimmer or large slotted spoon to carefully transfer the rosettes to the oil, three or four at a time to avoid crowding them. Use the skimmer to keep turning and pushing the rosettes down into the oil until they are golden all over, 2 to 3 minutes. As they are ready, transfer the rosettes to the baking sheet, inverting them over the pot of oil before transferring them to allow the oil to drain from the pockets. Continue until you have fried all of the rosettes.

To coat the *cartellate*, pour $1/2$ inch of *mosto cotto* or honey into a large skillet and warm it over medium heat just until it flows. Remove from the heat and place three to five rosettes into the syrup, or as many as can easily fit in a single layer. Use a spoon to baste the rosettes with the syrup, turning them over to generously cover all sides. The pockets will fill as you baste, but before removing them from the pan, invert the cartellate to let most of the syrup drain from the pockets. Transfer the *cartellate* right side up to a serving platter as you finish them. Continue to coat the remaining pastries. Sprinkle the tops with chopped nuts or *diavoletti* if you wish, then let cool completely.

Serve the *cartellate* at room temperature, storing leftovers, uncovered, for up to 24 hours.

Calzoncelli con i Ceci fried half-moon pastries with a chickpea-chocolate filling

Basilicata's *calzoncelli* are popular throughout Southern Italy, where they are called by various names: *canciuni* in Puglia, *chinule* in Calabria, and *panzarotti* in Campania. To make the Sicilian version, called *cassatelle,* fill the pastries with the ricotta filling used for cannoli (page 54) instead of the chickpea filling used here. Families, too, have their own variations, made by adding a couple of tablespoons of *mosto cotto* (page 197), *miele di fichi* (page 198), fig jam, espresso, or liqueur to the mixture, or by using a different type of nut.

In the mountains of Calabria and Basilicata, where chestnuts grow, they form the base for the filling. Some clever Southern Italian home cook must have realized that *ceci* (chickpeas) made a fine substitute where chestnuts do not grow, and after adding the chocolate, almonds, and other flavorings you would be hard pressed to detect the cook's secret.

To make the $2^{1}/_{2}$ cups of cooked, drained chickpeas needed for the recipe, cover 1 cup (200 g) of dried chickpeas with plenty of water and soak overnight at room temperature. Drain, cover with fresh water, and simmer until tender, 45 to 90 minutes, skimming any foam from the surface and adding water as needed to keep the chickpeas submerged. Cool the chickpeas completely in the liquid before draining and using.

These are best enjoyed warm, dusted with confectioners' sugar or drizzled with *mosto cotto* or honey.

PASTRY

- 3 cups (396 g) all-purpose flour, plus more for rolling the dough
- $^{1}/_{4}$ cup (50 g) granulated sugar
- 2 large eggs
- $^{1}/_{4}$ cup (60 ml) sweet or dry white wine
- 2 tablespoons light rum or other clear liqueur, such as anisette
- 2 tablespoons extra-virgin olive oil
- $^{1}/_{2}$ teaspoon pure vanilla extract

To make the dough, whisk together the flour and granulated sugar in a large bowl. Make a well in the center and add the eggs, wine, rum, oil, and vanilla. Use a fork to whisk the wet ingredients together, then begin mixing in the flour until it is all incorporated. You may want to use your hands at the end to bring the dough together.

Transfer the dough to a flat surface and knead until smooth, about 2 minutes. Wrap the dough in plastic wrap and refrigerate for at least 1 hour, or up to 4 hours, before forming the pastries.

To make the filling, process the chickpeas in a food processor until they are very finely chopped, about 1 minute. Add the honey and continue to process until smooth, scraping down the processor bowl as needed. Add the melted chocolate, Strega, cocoa, cinnamon, and orange zest; process to combine. Transfer the mixture to a bowl and stir in the almonds.

To form the pastries, divide the dough in quarters. Take one piece, leaving the remaining pieces covered, and flatten or roll the dough into a rectangle almost as wide as the slot of your pasta machine,

INGREDIENTS AND METHOD CONTINUED

FILLING

2¹/₂ cups (454 g) cooked, drained chickpeas (see headnote) or drained and rinsed canned chickpeas

¹/₂ cup (170 g) mild-flavored honey, such as clover or orange blossom

2 ounces (56 g) dark chocolate (about 55 to 65 percent cacao), melted

1 tablespoon Strega or other liqueur

1 tablespoon unsweetened Dutch-processed cocoa powder

¹/₄ teaspoon ground cinnamon

Finely grated zest of 1 orange

¹/₃ cup (50 g) almonds, toasted and finely chopped

Safflower or other neutral-tasting vegetable oil, for frying

Confectioners' sugar, for dusting, or mosto cotto (page 197) or honey, for drizzling

about 5 inches. Run the dough through the pasta machine the wide way, beginning with the widest setting and running it twice at each setting until you reach the second-to-narrowest setting, or the dough is ¹/₈ inch thick. Roll the dough only once at the final setting. As you work, keep the dough about the width of the machine and dust it lightly with flour only as needed to prevent sticking. (Alternatively, use a pin to roll the dough into a rectangle 25 inches by 5¹/₂ inches.)

Line a baking sheet with a clean kitchen towel. Lay out the dough strip on a lightly floured surface, gently stretching it if needed to about 25 inches by 5¹/₂ inches. Use a 4¹/₂-inch to 5-inch round cutter to cut out as many rounds as you can from the dough, cutting each one up against the last to make at least five rounds. Place 2 level tablespoons of the filling in the center of each round, forming it into a mound. Lightly brush the edge of the dough with water along the edge halfway around. Fold the dough over the filling to form a half-moon shape, pressing the dough closed all along the seam, then press the tines of a dinner fork all around the seam to tightly seal it. Transfer the filled pastries to the lined baking sheet as you form them.

Continue to roll, cut, and fill the remaining dough strips, including the one made up of collected scraps, to make a total of twenty-five *calzoncelli*. If you run slightly short of filling, cut the remaining dough into strips, fry, and dust with confectioners' sugar.) At this point, the *calzoncelli* are ready to fry and serve, or you can cover them with a kitchen towel and refrigerate for up to 8 hours before frying.

Fry the pastries shortly before serving them. Have ready a baking sheet lined with paper towels. Heat 2 inches of oil in a large, wide (4- to 6-quart) saucepan over medium-high heat to 375°F (190℃). Use a metal skimmer or large slotted spoon to carefully transfer the pastries to the oil, about three at a time to avoid crowding them. Use the skimmer or spoon to keep turning and pushing the pastries down into the oil until they are golden all over, 3 to 4 minutes.

As they are ready, allow the oil to drip back into the pot before transferring the pastries to the baking sheet to drain and cool for 15 to 30 minutes. By the time you have fried the last ones, the first should be cool enough to serve. Transfer them to a serving platter, dust generously with confectioners' sugar or drizzle with *mosto cotto* or honey, and serve warm.

Granita di Gelsi mulberry sorbet

In Southern Italy's hot summer months, you will find granita on display in a rainbow of flavors, with lemon, coffee, licorice, and almond milk being among the most popular. My personal favorite is made with *gelsi neri,* the native mulberries, and one of the best I've had was in Polignano a Mare (Puglia), made from the ripe berries sweetened with simple syrup.

If you are lucky enough to find a mulberry tree, look for plump berries that have turned from bright pink to inky purple—almost black—and give themselves up easily when you gently pull them from the branch. If you can't find these sweet gems, blackberries or olallieberries will do the job well.

Granita is named for the coarse grains of ice made by scraping up sweetened juice or flavored syrup as it freezes. These days, granita in Italy is almost always churned smooth, like *sorbetto,* though the name has stuck. If you don't have an ice cream machine, you can make it the old-fashioned way: Pour the granita mixture into a 13- by 9-inch glass baking pan and set it in a flat spot in the freezer. Wait an hour or so for it to begin to form ice crystals, then scrape with a fork every hour or so until the entire pan is filled with fine crystals, about 3 hours total. The scraped granita is best served within an hour or so after you finish scraping, while the crystals retain their fluffy texture.

³/₄ cup plus 2 tablespoons (175 g) granulated sugar

3 cups (720 ml) water

1¹/₄ pounds (568 g) fresh mulberries or blackberries (about 4 cups)

2 tablespoons fresh lemon juice

Make a simple syrup by heating the sugar with the water in a saucepan over low heat, stirring until the sugar dissolves. Cool to room temperature.

Pass the berries through a food mill. Alternatively, process them in a blender until nearly smooth and press them through a strainer to remove most of the seeds.

Add 1³/₄ cup purée to the simple syrup in the saucepan (save any remaining purée to use as a dessert sauce). Stir in the lemon juice.

Freeze the mixture in an ice cream maker according to the manufacturer's directions. Pack into an airtight container and freeze until firm enough to scoop, about 4 hours.

5

Master Recipes

The following basic recipes are referenced throughout the book. These are the go-to recipes used over and over again in desserts throughout Southern Italy. Making them yourself will save you the high price of purchasing imported products, if they can even be found, and will give you the best quality foundation for your desserts.

Pasta Frolla sweet short-crust pastry

This traditional Italian pastry dough has many uses, from forming the base for a rustic *crostata* (tart), to lining tarts, to creating a variety of cookies and pastries. Towns and even individual families each seem to put their own spin on the dough, varying proportions of butter or sugar, or adding vanilla or grated lemon or orange zest. My version produces a rich, flavorful tart dough that is easy to mix and handle. A bit of baking powder helps to crisp the crust as it bakes.

Look to the individual recipes throughout the book for instruction on whether to prepare the single- or double-crust version, as well as how to divide the dough for chilling and rolling.

INGREDIENT	SINGLE CRUST	DOUBLE CRUST
All-purpose flour	2 cups (264 g)	3 cups (396 g)
Granulated sugar	$^1/_2$ cup (100 g)	$^3/_4$ cup (150 g)
Baking powder	1 teaspoon	$1^1/_2$ teaspoons
Kosher salt	$^1/_4$ teaspoon	$^1/_4$ teaspoon
Unsalted butter	$^1/_2$ cup (113 g)	$^3/_4$ cup (170 g)
Eggs (large)	1 whole plus 1 yolk	2 whole
Finely grated lemon zest	1 teaspoon	$1^1/_2$ teaspoons

Combine the flour, sugar, baking powder, and salt in a food processor and pulse just a few times to combine them. Cut the butter into small cubes, about sixteen per stick, and add them to the food processor. Pulse until the butter is in small crumbs. Whisk the eggs (or egg and yolk) with the lemon zest in a small bowl. With the machine running, add the eggs through the feed tube. Mix, then pulse a few times, until the mixture comes together around the blade. When you stop the mixer and pinch it between your fingers, the dough should hold together easily.

Lay out a sheet of plastic wrap on a flat surface. Transfer the dough to the plastic wrap and press it together with your hands to form a smooth ball.

Flatten the dough into one or more disks (see specific recipes for instructions on dividing the dough), wrap tightly in plastic film, and refrigerate for at least 30 minutes, or up to 3 days, before rolling. Alternatively, you can place the wrapped disks into a ziplock bag and freeze for up to 1 month; thaw overnight in the refrigerator. If refrigerated for more than an hour, let stand, wrapped, at room temperature for 30 minutes before rolling.

Pan di Spagna sponge cake

Pan di Spagna, literally translated as "bread of Spain," really isn't from Spain at all. Rather, it originated in Genova, which is why the French refer to it as *génoise*. In Italy, the cake took its name after it was presented in the court of Spain. This is the only cake my mother makes, so in our home it is known as *torta della Nonna,* or grandmother's cake. You will find this universal cake used as a building block for desserts throughout Italy, and I've used it in many recipes in this book.

In my Calabrian childhood, with no electric mixer, making *pan di Spagna* was a laborious process. I would help my mom whip the eggs, which required 30 minutes of beating by holding two forks together, side by side, as a sort of make-shift whisk. When the rotary beater came on the scene shortly before we moved to the United States, we thought it was the best invention ever. In America, we graduated to a handheld electric mixer, reducing the whipping time to 20 minutes. With my stand mixer it takes just 15 minutes. What a long way we have come!

In addition to our limited tools, our home had no indoor oven—instead, we baked the cake in our wood-burning oven. We weren't permitted to walk near the oven lest the cake not rise, or worse, fall as it emerged. I am still in awe that we were able to bake those cakes with no thermometer to tell us the oven's temperature. Somehow, they always turned out perfectly.

It is essential that the eggs be at room temperature. Leave them (in their shells) out on the counter the night before, or submerge them in a bowl of warm water for 10 minutes. The cake can be prepared a day ahead and stored at room temperature, tightly wrapped.

3 large eggs, at room temperature

$^1/_2$ cup (100 g) granulated sugar

Finely grated zest of 1 lemon

$^3/_4$ cup (100 g) cake flour

Preheat the oven to 350°F (177°C) with a rack in the center of the oven. Butter a 9 by 2-inch round cake pan. Line the bottom with parchment paper, butter the parchment paper, then coat the pan with flour, knocking out the excess.

Beat the eggs and sugar in a stand mixer fitted with the whisk attachment for 15 minutes, starting at low speed and increasing to medium as they thicken. Mix in the lemon zest at low speed.

Remove the bowl from the mixer and sift the flour over the eggs in three additions, folding in each addition with a spatula just until it is incorporated. Be gentle: you don't want to deflate the eggs.

Gently spread the batter into the prepared pan and level the top. Bake until the cake is light golden and begins to pull away from the sides of the pan, 15 to 18 minutes. It should spring back when lightly pressed with a finger, and a toothpick should test clean if inserted at the center.

Transfer the pan to a wire rack to cool for 5 minutes, then run a knife around the edge of the pan and invert the cake directly onto the rack. Let the cake cool completely. Peel off the parchment paper before using.

Crema Pasticcera pastry cream

MAKES 1¹/₈ TO 2¹/₄ CUPS | GLUTEN FREE

When I make this rich cream using yolks from my backyard chickens, its deep yellow color transports me back to Calabria. If you have a friend who raises chickens, or know of a local farm where the chickens are pasture-raised, use their eggs for the richest color. However, this thick pastry cream is delicious no matter the eggs you use.

I grew up making this with whole milk, which is common throughout Italy. After trying it with various proportions of milk and cream, my favorite was with half-and-half, but you can make a good pastry cream with all whole milk, too. Cut the lemon peel in wide strips using a vegetable peeler, leaving behind the bitter white pith.

Use the table below to make the amount of pastry cream specified in the recipe.

INGREDIENT	YIELD		
	1¹/₈ cups (320 g)	1³/₄ cups (480 g)	2¹/₄ cups (640 g)
Half-and-half	1 cup (240 ml)	1¹/₂ cups (360 ml)	2 cups (480 ml)
Lemon peel	¹/₂ small lemon	1 small lemon	1 medium lemon
Egg yolks (large)	2	3	4
Granulated sugar	6 tablespoons (75 g)	¹/₂ cup + 1 Tbsp (113 g)	³/₄ cup (150 g)
Cornstarch	2 tablespoons (16 g)	3 tablespoons (24 g)	¹/₄ cup (32 g)

Bring the half-and-half and lemon peel to a simmer in a small saucepan; do not let it come to a full boil.

Meanwhile, in a 2- to 3-quart heavy, nonreactive saucepan, whisk the egg yolks and sugar until they are completely smooth and slightly thickened. Whisk in the cornstarch until it is completely incorporated.

Use a fork to carefully remove and discard the lemon peel from the half-and-half. Add the half-and-half to the egg mixture in a slow stream while whisking constantly. Return the mixture to medium heat and cook, whisking constantly, until the pastry cream boils. Continue to whisk as you boil the mixture for about 30 seconds to make a very thick cream—when you remove the whisk from the pan, you should have to shake or tap it firmly to drop a splotch of cream back into the pot.

Transfer the pastry cream to a bowl. To prevent a skin from forming, press a piece of plastic wrap directly onto the surface. Refrigerate until cold, about 4 hours, or up to 3 days. (To quickly chill the cream, fill a larger bowl with ice and water and set the bowl of pastry cream over it, taking care not to slosh water into the cream.)

Ricotta Fresca fresh ricotta

MAKES 4 TO 5 CUPS, ABOUT 2 POUNDS (900 G) | GLUTEN FREE

Until I moved to the United States, I had no idea how good I had it, with my father preparing a fresh batch of ricotta every day with the whey that remained from making pecorino—sheep's milk cheese. Ricotta means "recooked": the milk is first used to make pecorino, then the whey that remains is heated to coagulate its proteins into fresh curds for ricotta, typically consumed the day it is made.

Once you have tasted fresh, warm ricotta, scooped up with bread or spooned over fruit and drizzled with honey, you will have a hard time going back to the bland, industrially produced versions found on supermarket shelves. Luckily, it is easy to make with milk in place of whey. In Calabria, we made ours with rich sheep's milk. I've added a small amount of cream to approximate the richer texture and flavor, but it's not essential. In fact, the ricotta is very good, though not nearly as decadent, made with low-fat milk.

You need only a few supplies to make your own ricotta at home: fresh milk (the freshest, best quality you can find), liquid vegetable rennet, and two 2^1/$_2$-cup ricotta draining baskets or a 6-cup fine-mesh strainer. A digital thermometer will help you to keep the milk in the optimal temperature range for collecting the curds (see Sources, page 203, for cheese-making supplies).

1 gallon (about 4 L) whole milk

^{3}/$_4$ cup (180 ml) heavy cream

2 teaspoons kosher salt

^{1}/$_2$ teaspoon liquid vegetable rennet

^{1}/$_4$ cup (60 ml) cold water

Pictured on page 18

Stir together the milk and cream in a large, heavy pot over medium heat. Continue to heat until the milk foams and rises up in the pot. The milk should register 200° to 210°F (95° to 100°C) on an instant-read thermometer.

Carefully transfer the milk to a second large pot, leaving behind any bits of scorched milk at the bottom. (If you've been very careful to avoid scorching, you can skip this step.) Stir in the salt to dissolve it.

Let the milk cool until it registers 100°F (38°C), about 1 hour, or place the pot in a sink full of ice water to cool it more quickly, stirring occasionally to keep the temperature even, and taking care not to slosh water into the milk. As the milk cools, skim off any foam or skin that forms on top. Remove the milk from the ice bath as soon as it reaches the correct temperature.

In a small bowl, combine the rennet with the cold water. Stir diluted rennet into the milk and let it stand without stirring until the milk visibly thickens, about 10 minutes.

If you wish to follow the Italian tradition, use a wooden spoon to cut a large cross in the thickened milk to bless it, assuring a successful batch of ricotta. Stir the milk quickly with the wooden spoon to break up the coagulated milk, about 20 seconds. Switch to a metal skimmer and stir slowly in one direction, taking about 20 seconds to make one complete turn. As you stir, you will begin to see the milk separate into pillowy curds and thin, yellow-hued whey. Continue to stir slowly and gently, coaxing the curds toward the center of the pot, until you have a collection of curds in a sea of whey, about 5 minutes.

If using ricotta draining baskets, set them in shallow plastic containers or on a tray to drain. If using a fine-mesh strainer, set it over a bowl to drain.

Carefully pour the whey through a colander lined with cheesecloth to catch any small curds, gently holding back the curds with the skimmer. Use a spoon to gently transfer the ricotta to the baskets or strainer.

Let the ricotta stand at room temperature until whey no longer drips from the baskets or strainer, about 2 hours, discarding the whey periodically. Transfer the ricotta from the strainer to an airtight container for storage; nestle the baskets of ricotta snugly in a container or pan to catch any additional whey that drips out, covering tightly with a lid or plastic wrap. Use the ricotta immediately, or refrigerate for up to 3 days.

To serve the ricotta held in the baskets, invert the basket onto a plate. To use the ricotta in recipes, scoop it from the basket or container as needed.

Crema di Ricotta ricotta cream

MAKES ABOUT 2 CUPS (550 G) | GLUTEN FREE

This sweetened pressed ricotta is used in many recipes throughout the book. Use the finest screen you can find for sieving the ricotta. An ultrafine-mesh strainer will work in a pinch, but for the smoothest, creamiest ricotta cream, I press the ricotta through an ultrafine splatter screen (see page 14) using a firm but flexible plastic bowl scraper.

About 2 cups (454 g) fresh ricotta (page 186), well drained

$1/2$ cup (100 g) granulated sugar

$1/2$ teaspoon pure vanilla extract

Press the ricotta through an ultrafine-mesh strainer or splatter screen into a large bowl. Use a spatula to stir in the sugar and vanilla until well mixed. Cover and refrigerate overnight before using.

Mandorle Pelate blanched almonds

MAKES 1 CUP | GLUTEN FREE

Blanched almonds have been briefly boiled, allowing the skins to easily slip off. They are the almond of choice when you want to avoid the color or additional fiber and texture from the skin. Because I use them often, I find it easier and more cost-effective to purchase skin-on almonds in large quantities and blanch them myself. Often the skin-on nuts are fresher as well. This simple technique will free you from having to search out blanched almonds or pay extra for nuts that may not be as fresh.

Skinned hazelnuts are difficult to find and likewise command a premium price. Many people oven-roast the nuts and rub them in a towel to remove the skins. I find using this method infinitely easier and neater. For either almonds or hazelnuts, store the blanched nuts in an airtight container in the freezer.

1 cup (150 g) skin-on almonds

Bring 3 cups of water to a boil in a 2-quart saucepan. Add the nuts, bring the water back to a boil, and boil for 20 seconds longer.

Drain the almonds in a strainer and rinse them with cold water. When they are cool enough to handle, grab a nut and pinch from the larger, rounded end to poke out the nut—it will pop right out. Repeat to skin all of the almonds. Discard the skins.

Lay the nuts out on a baking sheet and let them dry completely before toasting, using in recipes, or storing in an airtight container. (Freeze for long-term storage.)

VARIATION: **Blanched Hazelnuts**

Bring 6 cups of water to a boil in a large (4-quart) saucepan. Stir 2 tablespoons of baking soda into the boiling water, then stir in 3 cups of skin-on hazelnuts. (Don't fret when the water foams up and turns black!) Bring the water back to a boil and boil for 3 minutes. To test that the nuts are blanched, fish out a nut with a slotted spoon and run it under cool water until you can easily handle it. If the skin slips off easily, they are ready; if not, boil a minute or two longer. Drain, rinse to cool, slip off the skins, dry, and use or store as above.

Pasta di Mandorla sweet almond paste

MAKES 1 GENEROUS CUP (350 G) | GLUTEN FREE

Maria Grammatico is a legendary Sicilian pastry maker with a fascinating story. She maintains a pastry shop high in the hills of Erice. Her pastries are largely centered around almond paste, the most commonly used ingredient in the area's sweets. Following World War II, Maria's mother sent her and her sister to the San Carlo convent in the hill town where she has remained since. There, under stark conditions, the sisters were schooled in producing the beautiful sweets sold to raise funds for the cloistered monastery that housed them. When she was released into the world as a young woman, Maria parlayed the only skill she knew into a celebrated pastry shop that continues to draw visitors from around the world. This is the recipe she shared with me.

You can easily find tubes of almond paste in the supermarket, but once you discover how easy it is to make yourself, you will certainly prefer this version, which allows you to ensure the freshness of the almonds and is considerably less expensive. Stored in the freezer, it will keep almost indefinitely.

1 cup (150 g) blanched almonds (page 189)

1 cup (200 g) granulated sugar

1/2 teaspoon pure almond extract

2 tablespoons water, plus 1 teaspoon if needed

Process the almonds with 2 tablespoons of the sugar in a blender or food processor to make as fine a powder as you can, occasionally pausing the blender to push the nuts down toward the blade. It should be between the texture of fine cornmeal and flour. Add the almond extract, water, and the remaining sugar and process to make a smooth paste. Add an additional teaspoon of water if needed to form the paste. Remove the paste from the blender and briefly knead it on a piece of plastic wrap, then wrap the paste tightly in the plastic. For long-term storage, freeze the wrapped paste in a ziplock bag; let thaw at room temperature for 1 hour before using.

Pasta di Pistacchio pistachio paste

MAKES 1 1/8 CUPS (250 G) | GLUTEN FREE

Similar to the other nut pastes, this one features the pistachios grown in Bronte, Sicily, and is used throughout the region. Another paste frequently found in the area is the sweetened, enriched *crema di pistacchio,* which is best purchased online (see Sources, page 203).

1 1/2 cups (200 g) raw shelled pistachios

6 tablespoons (90 ml) safflower or other neutral-tasting vegetable oil

Combine the nuts and oil in a blender and process until the paste is as smooth as you can get it, about the texture of creamy-style peanut butter. Refrigerate in an airtight container for up to 1 month.

Pasta di mandorla

Pasta di nocciola

Pasta di pistacchio

Pasta di Nocciola *hazelnut paste*

MAKES ABOUT 2 CUPS (480 G) | GLUTEN FREE

This flavorful nut paste is used in the Africano pastry (page 33) and La Deliziosa cookies (page 74). It's worth making enough to keep some on hand in your refrigerator—it is wonderful as a nut butter on toast. As an added bonus, my son Adrian has worked out a formula for a delicious chocolate hazelnut paste, homemade Nutella.

I find the easiest way to skin the nuts is by blanching (page 189). Alternatively, follow the recipe instructions below to toast the skin-on nuts, then wrap the warm nuts in a clean kitchen towel and rub vigorously to remove most of the skins before processing the warm nuts into a paste. You can purchase skinned nuts if you can find them.

3 cups (450 g) skinned hazelnuts (see headnote)

About 2 tablespoons safflower or other neutral-tasting vegetable oil, as needed

Pictured on page 191

Preheat the oven to 350°F (177°C). Spread out the nuts on a rimmed baking sheet and bake for 20 to 22 minutes, until they are very dark and almost smoking.

If you are using a powerful blender, such as a Blendtec or Vitamix, omit the oil unless you find you need it. For most blenders, or if using a food processor, pour in 2 tablespoons of oil, then add the warm hazelnuts. Process the nuts to make a smooth paste, occasionally scraping down the sides and pushing the nuts toward the blade as needed to keep them moving. Add a bit more oil only if needed to keep the mixture moving. Be persistent—it takes a little while to get the paste going, but once it does, it will quickly turn to a smooth paste.

VARIATION: **Chocolate-Hazelnut Paste**

$^2/_3$ cup (150 g) pasta di nocciola (hazelnut paste)

$^1/_2$ cup (63 g) confectioners' sugar

3 tablespoons unsweetened Dutch-processed cocoa powder

2 teaspoons safflower or other neutral-tasting vegetable oil

$^1/_4$ teaspoon pure vanilla extract

Stir the hazelnut paste, confectioners' sugar, cocoa, oil, and vanilla in a bowl until it is evenly blended. Refrigerate in an airtight container for up to 1 month; leave at room temperature for about 30 minutes to soften before using.

Scorze d'Arance Candite candied orange peel

MAKES ABOUT 35 PIECES | GLUTEN FREE

Each year in early spring, using the last oranges from our abundant backyard crop, I make candied orange peels to last throughout the year. What does not get used in cannoli, gelato, and other desserts will surely be enjoyed as candy, on its own or dipped in melted dark chocolate, or given to friends as holiday gifts. You can purchase candied orange peels, but they are costly and are never as good as homemade. Blanching the peels five times removes their bitterness and enhances their texture and flavor.

Choose organic fruit that has not been sprayed or coated with wax, because you'll be eating the peels. Segment the leftover orange flesh and add it to fruit salads, squeeze it for juice, or use it to make Marmellata di Arance (page 194).

5 large navel oranges with thick peels

4 cups (800 g) granulated sugar, plus more for coating

2 tablespoons fresh lemon juice

2 cups (480 ml) water

Use a paring knife to cut the peel from the orange, pith and all, in wide strips running from top to bottom. They will have an elongated diamond shape, about 1 inch at the widest point.

Put the peels into a large soup pot and cover them generously with cool water. Bring to a boil, boil for 2 minutes, and drain. Repeat the boiling and draining twice more. Return the peels to the pot, cover with cold water until cool enough to handle, then drain.

Lay one strip skin side down on a flat surface and use a paring knife running parallel to the rind to cut away most of the white pith inside, leaving about $1/8$ inch of pith along with the peel. Repeat with the remaining strips. (Discard the trimmings.) Return the peels to the pot, cover with cold water, and blanch two more times as before, for a total of five blanchings. Drain the peels and set aside.

Stir the sugar, lemon juice, and water in the pot. Bring to a boil and simmer for 15 minutes to slightly thicken the syrup. Add the peels and cook until they are shiny and translucent, about 1 hour. Remove the pot from the heat and let the peels plump in the syrup overnight.

Transfer the peels to a wire rack set over a rimmed baking sheet to dry. As you remove each peel from the syrup, run it between your thumb and forefinger to squeeze any excess syrup back into the pot. When the peels are no longer tacky—24 to 48 or more hours later—transfer the peels, a few at a time, to a shallow bowl of sugar, tossing to coat them well. Return the peels to the rack to dry overnight.

Transfer the peels to an airtight container with parchment paper separating the layers and store in the freezer, where they will keep for at least a year.

Marmellata di Arance orange marmalade

MAKES ABOUT 3 CUPS (720 ML) | GLUTEN FREE

Thick with chunks of fruit and strips of peel, this *marmellata* is like candied orange for your toast. Use organic—or at least pesticide-free—oranges that have not been waxed because the recipe includes the peels. Blanching them removes most of their bitterness, leaving a pleasantly sweet-tart marmalade. For blood orange marmalade use moro or other blood oranges.

The recipe is based on adding an equal weight of sugar to the peeled, chopped fruit. The fruit will weigh approximately $1^3/_4$ pounds. If you don't have a scale, 4 cups of sugar will get you close enough.

3 pounds (1.36 kg) navel or blood oranges (about 6 large)

Approximately 4 cups (800 g) sugar

2 tablespoons fresh lemon juice

Have ready three sterilized $^1/_2$-pint canning jars and lids, a ladle, and a wide-mouth funnel.

Use a vegetable peeler to remove the outer peel from three of the oranges in strips, taking the orange part only and leaving behind the bitter white pith. Set the peels aside.

For the remaining three oranges, use a sharp knife to cut off the tops and bottoms. Set one orange on a cut side on a cutting board, then work your way around the orange with a paring knife, cutting off the peel from top to bottom following the contour of the fruit, to remove and discard all of the peel and pith. Repeat to cut the peel and pith from the remaining two oranges, then remove the remaining pith from the three peeled oranges in the same manner; discard these peels and pith.

Cut all of the peeled oranges into $^1/_2$-inch-thick rounds. Lay the slices flat on the cutting board and cut them into strips the long way, then cut across the strips to make $^1/_4$-inch to $^1/_2$-inch slivers. Discard any seeds or white fibers from the center of the fruits as you go.

Weigh the chopped fruit—you should have a little under 2 pounds—and put it in a heavy, nonreactive 3-quart saucepan. (A wide, shallow saucepan will allow for faster evaporation as the *marmellata* cooks.) Add an equal weight of sugar, about 4 cups if you don't have a scale. Stir in the lemon juice and let stand for 30 minutes.

To blanch the peels, put them into a 1-quart saucepan and cover them generously with cool water—about 2 cups. Bring to a boil, boil for 2 minutes, then drain. Repeat the boiling and draining process until you have blanched the peels five times. After the last draining, put the peels back into the pot and cover with cool water. When they are cool enough to handle, drain them, then stack them on a cutting board, and cut them crosswise into thin strips, $^1/_8$ to $^1/_4$ inch wide. Add the strips to the oranges and sugar in the saucepan.

Bring the mixture to a boil over high heat, stirring frequently to prevent scorching or boiling over. Adjust the heat to cook at a moderate to lively boil, stirring occasionally, for 25 minutes, or until the *marmellata* has reached 220°F (104°C), before beginning to test for doneness (see sidebar). It will probably need a few minutes longer.

Taking care with the hot *marmellata,* immediately ladle it through the funnel into the jars, leaving about ¼ inch of space at the top. Wipe the rims clean and top with the lids. Turn the jars over on their heads on a flat surface and let them stand undisturbed until the jars are completely cool, up to 8 hours. You may hear the "pop" of the lids as they seal.

Check to see that the jars have sealed. (The little button on the lid will feel indented when you run your finger over it and it will not pop up or down when pressed.) Store sealed jars on a pantry shelf. Refrigerate any jars that have an unreliable seal, or after opening.

Because of the high proportion of sugar, I skip the step of processing these in a boiling water bath, an extra precaution against the growth of bacteria or mold. If you prefer to include this step, follow the USDA recommendations for processing the jars in a boiling water bath.

TESTING YOUR *MARMELLATA* FOR DONENESS

Before you begin making the *marmellata,* put a small dish into the freezer. After the mixture has boiled for 25 minutes or has reached 220°F (104°C), take out the plate, immediately spoon a teaspoon of *marmellata* onto it, and return the plate to the freezer for 2 to 3 minutes. Test by tipping the plate; if the jam runs, it needs a few minutes longer. It is ready when it barely travels, very slowly, down the plate. If you push it with your finger, it should bunch up and wrinkle a bit.

Mosto Cotto or Vino Cotto grape must or wine syrup

MAKES ABOUT 3 CUPS (720 ML) | GLUTEN FREE

Before sugar was widely available in Southern Italy, most families made their own sweetener by cooking grape must—the freshly pressed juice of wine grapes—into a thick syrup that added complex flavor as well as sweetness to their desserts. Because it is time consuming and expensive to produce, it is now difficult to find, even in Italy. *Mosto cotto* is sometimes incorrectly labeled as *vino cotto,* a similar syrup made from wine. In some regions of Italy, *mosto cotto* is known as *sapa.*

Whether made from grape must or wine, the syrup is thick and pourable, with flavors of fig, raisin, caramel, and spice, depending on the grapes used. It is perfect for drizzling over ice cream, fruit, or cheese, or for using in desserts, as is common throughout Southern Italy. Before the days of commercial ice cream, when fresh snow fell, Calabrians would pack it into a cup and drizzle it with the syrup for a treat known as *scirobetta.*

I make *mosto cotto* once a year, when we press grapes for making wine, and use it all year round. This recipe should leave you with enough for your own use, as well as some to package in small bottles to give as holiday gifts.

If you don't have access to fresh grape must from ripe, super-sweet wine grapes, or to juice bottled by a winery with no additives, make *vino cotto* instead: Mix a (750-ml) bottle of a fruity red wine, such as zinfandel, with 1 cup granulated sugar and follow the method below to cook and reduce the syrup to about 1 cup.

9$\frac{1}{2}$ cups (2.25 L) grape must

Strain the juice through a fine-mesh strainer into a large (6- to 8-quart) soup pot. Bring the juice to a boil over medium heat, skimming away any foam with a metal skimmer or spoon. Reduce to a lively simmer and cook, occasionally skimming off the foam, until dark amber and syrupy, about 2$\frac{1}{2}$ hours, reducing the heat and watching carefully toward the end to avoid scorching. Cool the syrup completely.

Strain the syrup through a fine-mesh strainer, then use a funnel to decant it into sterile bottles and seal. Store the *mosto cotto* in a cool, dark pantry, or refrigerate, for up to 1 year.

Miele di Fichi fig syrup

MAKES ABOUT 1 1/2 CUPS (360 ML) | GLUTEN FREE

Also known as *melazzo di fichi* (fig molasses) or *cotto di fichi,* this thick fig syrup is used throughout Southern Italy to sweeten and flavor desserts in place of sugar or honey. The recipe comes from Pietro Lecce, chef of the renowned restaurant La Tavernetta in Camigliatello, located in the La Sila Mountains, where he makes an exquisite gelato from the figs left from making the syrup.

In Calabria, we use the green Kadota figs (*ficho dottato*) that grow there, but you can use any light-colored fig, such as the Greek figs found pressed into round packages, or the Calimyrna variety. (The Greek ones often come in 14-ounce packages, in which case two packages, or 28 ounces, are enough to get the job done—no need to get a third just for the 4 extra ounces.) Until I discovered Chef Lecce's method, I made this the traditional way, using figs left to hang on the tree until they are fat, sagging, and deeply wrinkled, on their way to drying. The method is largely the same.

Don't discard the cooked figs: they will still have plenty of flavor. Enjoy them cut up in your breakfast cereal, with a piece of cheese, or thrown into your morning shake with milk, yogurt, and other fruits. To use them in the Gelato al Miele di Fichi (page 138), portion them into four ziplock bags, using 3/4 to 1 cup packed for each, and freeze. Thawed overnight, each bag will be enough for one batch of gelato.

About 2 pounds (900 g) dried figs

8 cups (2 L) water

Remove the stems from the figs and cut them in half. Put the figs in a large (6-quart) saucepan and cover them with the water. Bring to a boil, skim off any foam, then reduce the heat to a slow simmer. Cover, leaving the top slightly ajar to allow steam to escape, and cook until the figs are soft and the liquid is reduced by about half, about 3 hours.

Set a strainer lined with a few layers of cheesecloth over a large bowl and drain the figs, keeping the liquid. Draw up the ends of the cheesecloth, twist, and lay them over the figs, pressing down to compact them. Let stand until the figs are cool enough to handle and much of the syrup has dripped out, about 1 hour. When you can easily handle the figs, twist and press the cheesecloth, squeezing to extract as much of the liquid as you can. You should have 2 1/2 to 2 3/4 cups of syrup. (See headnote for ideas on using the figs.)

Transfer the syrup to a smaller saucepan and reduce over medium heat, uncovered, keeping it at a slow simmer, until it thickens and turns a dark caramel color, 40 to 50 minutes. Skim off and discard any foam as the syrup boils. When it is ready, the mixture should register 221°F (105°C) on a candy thermometer. When you put a spoonful onto a cold plate, it should run very little if at all. Once it reaches about 212°F (100℃), it may appear that the temperature will not budge; it will, but very slowly. Watch carefully during the last 10 minutes or so, as the syrup goes from a medium amber to a dark caramel color, taking care not to let it scorch or go much beyond the desired temperature.

Let the syrup cool completely, then transfer it to clean glass bottles, cover, and refrigerate. It should keep for many months.

Rosolio di Limone lemon liqueur

Limoncello is made in homes all over Southern Italy, where lemon trees grow in abundance. Less familiar outside Southern Italy is *rosolio di limone,* a lower-alcohol, sweeter variation of the liqueur that I find makes a better choice for using in desserts, such as Zabaione al Limoncello (page 97) and Biscotti di Ceglie (page 162).

To make limoncello, simply follow the instructions below, using 4 cups (1 L) of water and 2 cups (400 g) of sugar in place of the 6 cups of water and 4 cups of sugar below. An equal quantity of limoncello can be substituted for *rosolio di limone* in any of the recipes.

As a *digestivo* (after-dinner drink), both *rosolio* and limoncello are served cold; once you've opened a bottle, store it in the refrigerator or freezer. The alcohol will prevent it from freezing solid.

Here in California, I use Meyer lemons from my garden, but you can use any variety. If you purchase the lemons, look for ones that have not been sprayed or waxed, the fresher the better.

2 pounds lemons (about
   8 lemons)

1 bottle (750 ml) Everclear
   (151-proof) neutral grain
   spirits

4 cups (800 g) sugar

6 cups (1.5 L) water

Remove the peel from the lemons in strips with a vegetable peeler, taking only the yellow part and carefully avoiding even the slightest bit of white pith, which will turn the *rosolio* bitter.

Pour the alcohol into a clean quart (liter) jar with a tight-fitting lid, such as a European-style canning jar with a rubber gasket and clamp lid. Add the lemon peel. Close the jar and let steep for 1 week in a cool, dark place, such as a pantry or wine cellar.

After the alcohol has steeped, stir the sugar with the water in a large saucepan over low heat until the sugar dissolves completely. The mixture should be clear. Remove from the heat and let cool completely. (Do not be tempted to rush into the next step; if the sugar syrup is not completely cool, your rosolio will be cloudy.)

Remove the lemon peels from the alcohol (discard the peels) and pour the infused alcohol into the sugar syrup, stirring to combine. Pour the mixture through a fine-mesh strainer lined with cheesecloth, then decant the *rosolio* into clean bottles and seal with a cork or lid.

Let the *rosolio* mature for 15 days in a cool, dark place before using it, then refrigerate.

Sources

The following is a selection of products and brands mentioned in the book. Many of these items can also be found at general cookware stores and at Amazon.com.

Equipment

Baking sheets, bakeware, and cookware
www.allclad.com

Cake, tart, and springform pans; fluted brioche molds (for *bocconotti*); clear acetate cake wrap sheets
www.bakedeco.com

Cannoli forms
www.fantes.com

Ricotta draining baskets
www.cheesemaking.com

General and specialty cooking and baking equipment
www.cuisinart.com
www.kitchenaid.com
www.surlatable.com
www.williams-sonoma.com

Ingredients

Amarena Cherries
www.fabbrinorthamerica.com
www.markethallfoods.com
www.toschi.it

Candied citron, *crema di pistacchio*
www.markethallfoods.com

Candied orange peel, gelatin sheets, nut flours, nut pastes
www.lepicerie.com

Cheese making: liquid rennet
www.cheesemaking.com

Chocolate: Valrhona cocoa powder and chocolate
www.chocosphere.com
www.lepicerie.com
www.valrhona.com

***Confettura di peperoncini* (Calabrian hot pepper jam)**
www.taylorsmarket.com
www.tuttocalabria.com

Flour, food coloring, gelatin sheets
www.kingarthurflour.com

Licorice: Amarelli brand *liquirizia spezzata*, from Calabria
www.smallflower.com

Liqueurs: Strega, Luxardo Maraschino, limoncello, anisette
www.bevmo.com

***Miele di fichi* (fig syrup; also sold as *melazzo di fichi*)**
www.markethallfoods.com
www.ilmercatoitaliano.net

Mosto cotto (vino cotto)
www.vinocotto.us

Orange extract
www.flavorganics.com
www.markethallfoods.com

Ricotta
www.angeloandfranco.com
www.bellwetherfarms.com
www.calabrocheese.com

Bibliography

The following are books I referenced while writing this book or that provide useful information about the desserts of Southern Italy.

Bordo, V., and A. Surrusca. *L'Italia dei dolci. Guida alla scoperta e alla conoscenza.* Bra: Slow Food, 2003.

Cafiero, Antonio. *Sorrento e le sue Delizie.* Sorrento: Franco di Mauro Editore, 1999.

De Riso, Salvatore. *Dolci del Sole.* Milano: Rizzoli, 2009.

Di Leo, Maria Adele. *I dolci Siciliani.* Roma: Newton & Compton, 2004.

Granof, Victoria. *Sweet Sicily: The Story of an Island and Her Pastries.* NY: Regan Books, 2001.

Lazari, Lucia. *1000 Ricette di Puglia.* Milano: Congedo Publishing, 2011.

Limatora, Guglielmo. *Antica Pasticceria Napoletana.* Napoli: Edizioni EDI PRINT, 2005.

Malgieri, Nick. *Great Italian Desserts.* NY: Little, Brown and Co., 1990.

Martina, Franco. *La Cucina del Parco.* Bari: Edizioni Giannatelli, 2009.

Simeti, Mary Taylor. *Pomp and Sustenance: Twenty-five Centuries of Sicilian Food.* NY: Knopf, 1989.

Simeti, Mary Taylor, and Maria Grammatico. *Bitter Almonds: Recollections and Recipes from a Sicilian Girlhood.* NY: Bantam Books, 1994.

Conversion Charts

VOLUME

U.S.	Imperial	Metric
1 tablespoon	$^1/_2$ fl oz	15 ml
2 tablespoons	1 fl oz	30 ml
$^1/_4$ cup	2 fl oz	60 ml
$^1/_3$ cup	3 fl oz	90 ml
$^1/_2$ cup	4 fl oz	120 ml
$^2/_3$ cup	5 fl oz ($^1/_4$ pint)	150 ml
$^3/_4$ cup	6 fl oz	180 ml
1 cup	8 fl oz ($^1/_3$ pint)	240 ml
1$^1/_4$ cups	10 fl oz ($^1/_2$ pint)	300 ml
2 cups (1 pint)	16 fl oz ($^2/_3$ pint)	480 ml
2$^1/_2$ cups	20 fl oz (1 pint)	600 ml
1 quart	32 fl oz (1$^2/_3$ pints)	1 L

TEMPERATURE

Fahrenheit	Celsius/Gas Mark
250°F	120°C/gas mark $^1/_2$
275°F	135°C/gas mark 1
300°F	150°C/gas mark 2
325°F	160°C/gas mark 3
350°F	175°C/gas mark 4
375°F	190°C/gas mark 5
400°F	200°C/gas mark 6
425°F	220°C/gas mark 7
450°F	230°C/gas mark 8
475°F	245°C/gas mark 9
500°F	260°C

LENGTH

Inch	Metric
$^1/_4$ inch	6 mm
$^1/_2$ inch	1.25 cm
$^3/_4$ inch	2 cm
1 inch	2.5 cm
6 inches ($^1/_2$ foot)	15 cm
12 inches (1 foot)	30 cm

WEIGHT

U.S./Imperial	Metric
$^1/_2$ oz	15 g
1 oz	30 g
2 oz	60 g
$^1/_4$ lb	115 g
$^1/_3$ lb	150 g
$^1/_2$ lb	225 g
$^3/_4$ lb	350 g
1 lb	450 g

Index

Ten Speed Press and the Ten Speed Press colophon are registered trademarks of
Random House, Inc.

Library of Congress Cataloging-in-Publication Data

Costantino, Rosetta.
  Southern Italian desserts / Rosetta Costantino ; with Jennie Schacht ; photographs by Sara
Remington.
    pages cm
  Includes bibliographical references.
1. Desserts. 2. Cooking, Italian—Southern style 3. Cookbooks. I. Schacht, Jennie. II.
Remington, Sara. III. Title.
  TX773.C6366 2013
  641.86—dc23
                        2012046952

Hardcover ISBN: 978-1-60774-402-3
eBook ISBN: 978-1-60774-403-0

Printed in China

Design by Betsy Stromberg
Food Styling by Katie Christ
Prop Styling by Dani Fisher

10 9 8 7 6 5 4 3 2 1

First Edition